Clodagh's Kitchen Diaries

Clodagh McKenna

Clodagh's Kitchen Diaries

Delicious recipes throughout the year

Clodagh McKenna

Kyle Books

Published in 2013 by
Kyle Books
an imprint of Kyle Cathie Ltd.
www.kylebooks.com

Distributed by National Book Network
4501 Forbes Blvd., Suite 200
Lanham, MD 20706
Phone: (800) 462-6420

10 9 8 7 6 5 4 3 2 1

ISBN 978-1-906868-86-4

Clodagh McKenna is hereby identified as the
authors of this work in accordance with
Section 77 of the Copyright, Designs, and
Patents Act 1988.

Text © 2012 Clodagh McKenna
Book design © 2012 Kyle Books Limited
Photography © 2012 Kate Whitaker, except
page 277 © Ruth Monahan

Project editor: Emma Bastow
Designer: Lucy Parissi
Home economist: Lizzie Harris
Prop stylist: Penny Markham
Production: Gemma John and Nic Jones

Library of Congress Control Number:
2012953412

Color reproduction by ALTA London
Printed in China by C&C Offset Printing Co.,LTD

CONTENTS

INTRODUCTION

As I write this book I think to myself, so why a diary? Well, the last few years it has felt like someone pressed fast forward on my life. I am always on the move. I love change and new experiences, and luckily for me my work is all about that. The only thing is, with the frantic pace I do forget details of these wonderful experiences. Last year was no exception with the opening of my Homemade Food Court, Clodagh's Kitchen Restaurant and my Bakery in Dublin; trips to America to promote my TV series *Clodagh's Irish Food Trails*; the cookery school classes and in-store demonstrations; all alongside the regular day-to-day work. The diary started as an itinerary-come-memory-aid but has ended up being so much more.

I have always associated memorable events and times in my life with food. I remember family birthdays by the cakes my mother baked and holidays by the local food we ate. As food is the filter through which I see and understand the world, it made sense for my diary to take the form of a food journal.

I have been keeping the journal for a couple of years now and it is incredibly useful for looking back and taking stock, and also for planning forward.

Flicking back through last year's pages I get a real sense of the changing seasons and the availability of certain foods in particular months. It's great to look back to January when I need a bit of motivation to keep healthy. A makeover might be a great short term pick-me-up, but feeding yourself well is a fundamental way of increasing your wellbeing in the long term. The January chapter is packed with great tasting superfood recipes to keep you on track throughout the year.

Planning ahead I notice how much of the seasonal celebrations, holidays, and occasions with friends and family center around food. I've included menu plans for Christmas, Easter, New Year and, of course, Valentine's. I love the sense of upholding these traditions with a meal. It binds people together and gives us a sense of continuity.

So, back to my original question: why a diary? Reading back over last year I realise it is not just a record of meals eaten or events attended. Each page is filled with memories of the people I celebrated and shared food with and the wonderful places I have lived and eaten in, from Dublin, London, NYC, Italy, and France. Here's to another great year and many more meals to come.

Roasted Thyme Turkey

Homemade Cinnamon, Pumpkin, and Cranberry Granola

JANUARY

SUPERFOODS

Are you one of those people who, after a couple of thoroughly indulgent nights... weeks... maybe months... resolves to turn your life around? You will eat only whatever the fashionable superfood of the moment is and start achieving optimal performance from your body and mind, starting Monday. Then Monday passes and you promise to do it from the first of the next month. That deadline slips and now you're focussing on the first of January. Sound familiar? Me too.

I read an article about celebrity relationships with food. One very fit celebrity said she didn't "eat for pleasure," that food was simply "fuel for my body." Wow! I would describe my relationship with food as a full blown love affair, one of the great joys in my life. That's when I realized my problem with these superfood diets—I need food to taste great. I think taste is my strongest sense and it just wasn't tempted by the very healthy, but very unappetizing, superfood meals available.

Then, at the end of last year I watched a great friend of mine, an avid gym-goer, order the most indulgent meal on the menu. I commented that it made all his work in the gym meaningless. He laughingly replied, "Clo, you've got it the wrong way round. I go to the gym so that I can eat like this." It was a real light bulb moment for me—the ying and yang of eating. If I ate enough of the good stuff—the fiber, the greens, the all-important antioxidants— then I could treat myself to the filet mignon and the glass of Burgundy I occasionally craved.

So, at the end of last year I resolved that from the 1st of January I was going to go for it. I embraced the superfoods but I used them in delicious recipes to keep me motivated. And guess what, very quickly I started to feel a whole lot better. I'm an active, sporty girl and I work hard. Yes, I need my energy tank fueled but I also need my taste buds tickled. This chapter is filled with recipes using powerfoods without the punishment. Delicious, healthy meals that make you feel great about yourself. Oh and another bonus, I've stuck to my New Year's resolution and it is July when I'm writing this! Easy when eating is about pleasure not denial.

HOMEMADE CINNAMON, PUMPKIN, AND CRANBERRY GRANOLA

No store-bought granola can compare to a homemade version, eaten fresh from the oven, still a little warm and melting into your yogurt.

Makes 2¼ lb

6½ tablespoons butter

1 teaspoon ground cinnamon

⅔ cup honey

1 teaspoon vanilla extract

1 lb 2 oz rolled oats

1⅓ cups hazelnuts, roughly chopped

¾ cup pumpkin seeds

¾ cup sunflower seeds

¾ cup unsweetened coconut flakes

2 cups mixed dried fruit (apricots, golden raisins, raisins, cranberries)

Preheat the oven to 350°F.

Melt the butter, cinnamon, honey, and vanilla extract in a small saucepan.

Put the oats, nuts, seeds, and coconut flakes in a large bowl and pour over the melted butter and honey mixture. Stir well so that all the dry ingredients are evenly coated.

Transfer the mixture to two large baking sheets and cook in the oven for 20 minutes, or until golden brown, tossing every 5 minutes.

Remove from the oven and leave to cool on the sheets, stirring every few minutes.

Delicious served with low-fat yogurt and fresh berries.

BLUEBERRY, CINNAMON, AND FLAXSEED OATMEAL

Buy a big bag of flaxseed for your pantry. I use the Linwoods brand—they make a fantastic mixture with goji berries.

Serves 2

¾ cup water or fat-free milk

⅔ cup organic jumbo oats

1 teaspoon ground cinnamon

3½ oz fresh blueberries

½ banana, sliced

1 tablespoon ground flaxseed

Put a saucepan over medium heat and pour in the water or milk (or half of each). Stir in the oats and cook for 5 minutes, stirring occasionally.

Stir in the cinnamon, blueberries, banana, and flaxseed, and cook for a further minute and serve.

OAT AND CINNAMON HEALTH MUFFINS

Ok, so there is a little brown sugar in this otherwise healthy muffin recipe, but it's a ying-yang muffin!

Makes 8

1¼ cups self-rising flour

1 teaspoon baking soda

⅔ cup oats

1 cup brown sugar

2 teaspoons ground cinnamon

½ cup fat-free milk

6 tablespoons sunflower oil

⅓ cup golden raisins

½ cup walnuts, chopped

Preheat the oven to 350°F. Line a muffin pan with 8 paper baking cups.

Sift the flour and baking soda into a large bowl and stir in the oats, sugar, and cinnamon. Stir in the milk and oil, then fold the raisins and walnuts into the mixture.

Spoon the mixture into the paper cups, filling them to the brim, and bake in the oven for 20-25 minutes until risen and golden. Serve warm or at room temperature.

CHORIZO AND TOMATO BAKED EGGS

Super simple to make and there are tons of ways
to vary this recipe. Try adding pancetta or sausage,
or whatever you fancy.

Serves 2

2 tablespoons butter
4 eggs
3 cherry tomatoes,
halved
½ cup Gruyère cheese
(or another hard cheese,
such as Cheddar or
Gouda), grated
1 teaspoon mustard
1 in chorizo, finely
diced
1 tablespoon heavy cream
sea salt and freshly
ground black pepper
slices of bread,
toasted, to serve

Preheat the oven to 350°F.

Grease 2 small ovenproof dishes with the
butter and crack 2 eggs into each one.
Arrange the tomatoes around the eggs.

Put the cheese in a small bowl and mix with
the mustard, chorizo, and cream. Season with
salt and pepper. Scoop the cheese mixture
on top of the eggs and bake in the oven
for 10 minutes.

Serve with toasted bread cut into thin slices
so that you can dip them into the eggs.

EGGS FLORENTINE ON TOASTED SESAME BAGELS

Freshly-poached eggs on a toasty bed snuggled up in a blanket of creamy hollandaise. Is there a better way to start the day?

Serves 2

2 eggs

7 oz baby spinach, steamed and drained on paper towels

sesame bagels, cut in half and toasted

$1/2$ cup hollandaise sauce (see page 91)

sea salt and freshly ground black pepper

There are a couple of tricks to making perfect poached eggs, but for both you should put a large saucepan of cold salted water over high heat and bring to a boil. When the water is at a rolling boil, stir vigorously with a spoon. While the water is swirling, bring your hands as close as you can to the top of the saucepan and crack your egg into the swirling hot water, which helps bring the egg together. Some people add vinegar, but I prefer the swirling method. Alternatively, you can also crack your egg into a cup and tip it into the boiling water. Allow the eggs to poach for 3 minutes. Once the egg has poached, remove it with a slotted spoon and rest on paper towels for 30 seconds to drain the excess water.

Spoon the steamed spinach on top of the toasted bagels, followed by the poached eggs and then cover with lots of hollandaise sauce. Season with salt and pepper.

OMELET FOR ONE

I once stayed in a fishing lodge in Cavan, Ireland, and the wonderful German owner used to make me an omelet every morning. He made it thin and added slices of German salami and Gruyère cheese, to set us up for our day on the lake. I also love a cold omelet, sandwiched in sourdough with lots of homemade mayonnaise.

Serves 1

2 large eggs

⅔ cup mature Cheddar cheese, grated

½ scallion, finely sliced

2 teaspoons olive oil

⅔ cup mushrooms, sliced (optional)

2 bacon slices, chopped (optional)

¼ red pepper, seeded and diced (optional)

3 cherry tomatoes, halved

sea salt and freshly ground black pepper

green salad, to serve

Preheat the oven to 350°F.

Crack the eggs into a mixing bowl and whisk vigorously. Add the cheese and scallion and season with salt and pepper. Whisk again.

Put a nonstick ovenproof pan over medium heat and add the oil. Swirl the hot oil around the pan and turn up the heat. If you are adding mushrooms, bacon, or red pepper, add them to the pan now and cook for 2 minutes before adding the egg. Add in the egg mixture, swirling it around the pan to make sure it covers all the pan.

Put the halved cherry tomatoes on one side of the omelet and cook in the oven for 5 minutes. Remove from the oven and use a spatula to flip one side of the omelet on top of the other half and slide onto a plate. I like to eat my omelet with a green salad.

HUMMUS, TZATZIKI, AND CILANTRO WRAP

If you are taking this to work for lunch, I would suggest you assemble it just before eating. Salty feta is a delicious addition to this wrap, and if you don't like cilantro you can replace with fresh arugula.

Serves 2

2 flour wraps
(use spinach wraps
if you can)

3 tablespoons hummus
(see page 166)

3 tablespoons tzatziki
(see page 166)

2 sprigs of fresh
cilantro, finely chopped

$^1/_4$ cucumber, finely
sliced

$3^1/_2$ oz salad leaves

Lay the wraps out flat. Divide the remaining ingredients equally between them, placing them down the middle of the wraps. Roll up the wraps and serve.

BLUEBERRY SUPERFOOD SALAD

Sweet, sweet blueberries. So good for you, and so delicious combined with celery, apple, orange, and pomegranate for a super tasty, wholesome salad.

Serves 4

3 tablespoons extra virgin olive oil

1 tablespoon balsamic vinegar

3½ oz fresh blueberries

1⅓ cups feta cheese, crumbled

1 apple, grated

2 celery ribs, finely sliced

1 orange, peeled and segments quartered, retaining the juice

seeds of 1 pomegranate

½ cup walnuts, toasted and finely chopped

Whisk together the oil and vinegar.

Put the remaining ingredients in a bowl, mix together, and pour the dressing over the salad. Toss well and serve.

POWER ME SALAD

This is the number one selling salad in my restaurants. Packed with flavor yet light and nutritious, it's the perfect antidote to the party season.

Serves 2

1 apple, grated
1 carrot, grated
1 beet, grated
1/2 fennel, grated
3 1/2 oz salad leaves
1/2 cup canned chickpeas, rinsed and drained
juice and zest of 1 orange
juice and zest of 1 lime
3 tablespoons extra virgin olive oil
1/2 cup pumpkin seeds, toasted
sea salt and freshly ground black pepper

Put the grated apple and vegetables, salad leaves, and chickpeas in a mixing bowl. Add the juice and zest of the orange and lime along with the olive oil. Season with salt and pepper and toss well. Sprinkle the toasted pumpkin seeds on top and serve.

MOROCCAN SPICED LENTIL SOUP

Serves 6

2 teaspoons olive oil

1 onion, finely diced

2 garlic cloves, crushed

4-in piece of fresh ginger, peeled and grated

1⅓ quarts water

1 cup red lentils

14-oz can chickpeas, rinsed and drained

14-oz can cannellini beans, rinsed and drained

14-oz can chopped tomatoes

1 large carrot, finely diced

1 large celery stalk, finely diced

1 teaspoon garam masala

1 teaspoon ground cardamom

½ teaspoon ground cayenne pepper

½ teaspoon ground cumin

sea salt and freshly ground black pepper

With a well stocked pantry, this will soon become one of your feed-me-and-make-me-feel-good soups.

Put a large saucepan over medium heat and add the oil. Stir in the onion, garlic, and ginger and allow to simmer for 5 minutes.

Add the water, lentils, chickpeas, cannellini beans, tomatoes, carrots, celery, garam masala, cardamom, cayenne pepper, and cumin. Bring to a boil and allow to boil rapidly for a few minutes, then reduce the heat and simmer for 1-1½ hours or longer until the lentils are soft. Taste and season with salt and pepper if needed.

If you want a more rustic soup leave it as is; otherwise, blend in a food processor for a smoother consistency.

NUTMEG AND POTATO PANCAKES

Try serving these pancakes alongside meaty, herby sausages and homemade ketchup for a different take on sausage and mashed potatoes.

Serves 4

1 lb potatoes, peeled
and grated

1 medium onion, grated

2 1/2 teaspoons freshly
ground nutmeg

2 tablespoons
all-purpose flour

1 egg, lightly beaten

1 1/2 tablespoons
sunflower oil

sea salt and freshly
ground black pepper

Toss together the potatoes, onion, nutmeg, flour, and egg in a large bowl. Season to taste with salt and pepper.

Heat ¾ tablespoon of the oil in a large, nonstick grill pan or frying pan over medium-high heat. Drop 3 tablespoons of the potato mixture (1 per pancake) into the pan. Flatten each pancake with a nonstick spatula. Reduce the heat to medium-low and cook for about 5 minutes on each side until they are golden brown. Transfer to a plate lined with paper towels and keep warm. Repeat, using all the batter and adding additional oil as needed. Serve warm.

ROASTED THYME TURKEY WITH SWEET POTATOES AND ROASTED BEETS

Many of us tend to only eat turkey at the holidays, but it's an excellent source of lean protein and contains the trace mineral selenium as well as niacin and vitamin B6. Selenium supports the immune system while niacin and Vitamin B6 aid energy production. So there you have it, turkey is a winner all-around.

Serves 4

2¼ lb rolled and boned turkey

4 tablespoons olive oil

leaves from 2 sprigs of thyme

about 4 beets, scrubbed

1 teaspoon balsamic vinegar

6 sweet potatoes, peeled

1 teaspoon ground cumin

sea salt and freshly ground black pepper

Preheat the oven to 400°F. Take the turkey out of the fridge and allow it to come to room temperature. Put the turkey into a roasting pan and season with salt and pepper. Mix 1 tablespoon of the olive oil with the thyme leaves, spread the oil over the turkey, and cook in the oven for 1 hour. (This is 15 minutes for each pound of turkey, plus an additional 25 minutes.)

Cut the beets into large cubes or wedges and put them in a bowl with 1 tablespoon of the oil and the balsamic vinegar. Season with salt and pepper, transfer to a roasting pan, and cook in the oven for 25 minutes.

Cut the sweet potatoes into wedges and put them in a bowl with the remaining oil and the ground cumin, and season with salt and pepper. Remove the beets from the oven after they have been cooking for 5 minutes and mix in the sweet potatoes. Return the pan to the oven and cook the sweet potatoes and beets for a further 20 minutes or until cooked.

Allow the cooked turkey to rest for 10 minutes before slicing; if necessary, keep it warm by covering it with a tent of aluminum foil. Serve with my delicious Spiced Cranberry Sauce (see page 300).

PAN-ROASTED LEMON AND BASIL SALMON

Also delicious made with cod, halibut, or any other fish in season in your part of the world.

Serves 2

2 salmon fillets
8 basil leaves
1 lemon, thinly sliced
3 tablespoons olive oil
or canola oil
sea salt and freshly
ground black pepper

Preheat the oven to 350°F.

Cut the salmon fillets lengthwise two-thirds of the way through the center and open them up. Put 4 basil leaves along the length of each of the opened fillets and put 2-3 slices of lemon on top of the basil. Season with salt and pepper and close the fillets.

Heat a griddle or frying pan over medium heat, add the oil, and swirl it around to coat the pan. Carefully place the salmon, skin side down, in the pan and cook for 3 minutes. Turn the fillets over and put the remaining slices of lemon on top of the salmon. Transfer to the oven and cook for 10 minutes.

The salmon is delicious served with a green salad and Avocado and Beet Salsa (see below).

AVOCADO AND BEET SALSA

Serves 4

1 avocado, peeled, pit
removed, and diced
1/2 red onion, finely
chopped
1 1/4 cups cooked beets,
diced
juice of 1 lime
1 tablespoon balsamic
vinegar
2 tablespoons extra
virgin olive oil
sea salt and freshly
ground black pepper

Put all the ingredients into a bowl and mix well. Season with salt and pepper.

Put the pit of the avocado in with the salsa, cover with plastic wrap, and store in a fridge. The pit will keep the avocado from turning gray in color.

BRIOCHE

The smell of fresh brioche wafting from the kitchen is the most incredible aroma. Enjoy with lots of lemon curd, rhubarb jam, or crispy bacon and maple syrup.

Makes 2 loaves

½ cup warm water
1 teaspoon active dry yeast
3¼ cups all-purpose flour, plus extra for flouring
1 teaspoon salt
2 teaspoons white granulated sugar
4 eggs, lightly beaten
½ lb butter, softened

For the glaze

1 egg yolk
1 teaspoon cold water

Preheat the oven to 400°F.

Put the water and the yeast in a bowl and whisk together. Leave for 10 minutes until frothy.

Sift the flour into a large mixing bowl and add the salt and sugar. Make a well in the center and mix in the eggs and the yeast mixture. Beat well until the dough has come together, then turn it out on to a lightly floured surface and knead for about 8 minutes until smooth and supple.

Flatten the dough and spread it with one-third of the butter. Knead this well. Repeat this twice to incorporate the remaining butter, allowing the dough to rest for a few minutes between the additions of butter. This process may take 20 minutes or so. Lightly oil a large bowl, place the dough into the bowl, and turn to coat with oil. Cover with plastic wrap and leave in a warm place for about 1 hour until it has doubled in volume.

Punch down the dough, cover with plastic wrap, and refrigerate for
6 hours or overnight. It needs time to chill in order to become
more workable.

Lightly grease two 2-lb loaf pans. Turn the dough out onto a lightly
floured surface and divide it into two equal pieces. Form the pieces into
loaves and place them in the prepared pans. Cover with greased plastic
wrap and leave to rise for about 1 hour until doubled in volume.

Beat the egg yolk with 1 teaspoon of water to make a glaze and brush
over the loaves using a pastry brush. Bake for 25 minutes or until the
loaves are deep golden brown. Allow the loaves to cool in their pans for
10 minutes before removing to wire racks to cool completely.

HEALTH LOAF

This is my Aunt Muriel's recipe. It has now become our house bread in my restaurants and hopefully will in your home, too!

Preheat the oven to 450°F.

Makes 2 loaves

1 lb whole-wheat flour

²⁄₃ cup wheatgerm, plus extra for dusting

½ cup all-purpose flour

1¼ cups wheat bran

1⅓ cups steel-cut oats

2 teaspoons brown sugar

2 teaspoons bread soda or baking soda

1 quart buttermilk

For the topping

2 teaspoons wheatgerm, plus extra for dusting

2 teaspoons sesame seeds

Put all of the dry ingredients into a large bowl and mix together. Stir in the buttermilk to make a moist dough.

Lightly grease two 2 lb loaf pans and dust them with wheatgerm. Divide the dough between the pans, smooth the top, and make a cross on each one with a floured knife. Sprinkle with wheatgerm and sesame seeds.

Cook the loaves in the oven for 10 minutes, then reduce the temperature to 250°F and bake for 1 hour.

When the loaves are cooked, remove from the oven and leave in the pans to cool a little, then turn them out onto wire racks to cool completely.

GREEN DETOX JUICE

I do my best to get to my friend Oliver McCabe's Select Stores in Dalkey, Dublin, once a week for his Green Detox Juice. I always feel wonderful afterward. This juice is fantastic for detoxifying and cleansing the system, and if you are on a serious health plan I would suggest you have this every morning to start your day.

Serves 1

3 apples

½ cucumber

handful of spinach

small bunch of parsley

dash of wheatgrass or spirulina

Juice the apples, cucumber, spinach, and parsley and add the wheatgrass or spirulina. Pour into a chilled glass and enjoy.

SUPERFOOD SNACK MIX

Last year I started to leave little bowls of raw,
unsalted and unsweetened nut and dried fruit mixes
around the house and office, so that when I was hungry I
could reach for an energy-boosting snack rather than
chocolate bars that just give me a high and then slow me
down. You can mix any of the nuts and dried fruits
listed below (keep clear of raisins because they contain
a lot of natural sugars) and if you are having a
chocolate craving add a square of good quality dark
chocolate with cocoa solids above 70 percent.

walnuts
whole almonds
hazelnuts
pumpkin seeds
sunflower seeds
goji berries
dried unsweetened
cranberries
dried unsweetened
blueberries
acai berries

Use whatever quantities or combinations of the nuts
and fruit you like. Simply stir gently to combine and
divide into bowls or airtight containers, then keep a
stash in your handbag or desk drawer for an instant
energy boost.

BLOOD ORANGE MIMOSAS

The flavor of blood oranges in place of regular oranges in this mimosa is really something special, and the color is so inviting. A great pick-me-up to combat the January blues.

Serves 8

1½ cups freshly squeezed blood orange juice

1 bottle of chilled dry prosecco

red blood orange segments, to garnish (optional)

Fill 8 Champagne flutes one-third full with blood orange juice and top up with prosecco.

Garnish with a segment of blood orange, if liked, and serve. A great way to cheer-up a dreary January weekend.

Skinny Fries

Red Velvet Cupcakes

FEBRUARY

VALENTINE'S DAY

One Valentine's weekend, I was instructed to pack my suitcase and have my passport ready. It was only when we reached the boarding gate that I knew we were en route to Paris. Two hours later I was tucked away in Le Bar of The George V hotel, sipping on a brandy and Champagne cocktail, pinching myself to make sure I wasn't dreaming. The great cities of the world all have their own spirit; New York buzzes with ideas, London is both regal and irreverent, but there is only one word for Paris: romantic. I was living the dream.

The next morning we walked from the lavish George V to the red banquettes and mahogany tables of Café de Flore on the Left Bank. We sat where Satré and Camus used to sit and ordered the famous *Jambon et Fromage* omelet. We spent hours alternating between coffee and pastis, just watching the world go by. From a famous coffeehouse to the famous salon de thé Ladurée on Champs-Élysées, well-known for making the first and best macaroons in the world. They were like Paris itself; elegant, exquisite, and hopelessly romantic.

We can't all catch a plane to Paris but we can all recreate the romantic atmosphere. Pop a truffle in your lover's pocket when they leave for work. In the afternoon send him or her a menu card for dinner via a pic on your phone. Light candles, put perfume in your hair, and play something French. Have everything prepared beforehand so that you can give them your undivided attention and a delicious cocktail when they arrive. And sweet nothings sound so much more romantic whispered in French—*Que mes baisers soient les mots d'amour que je ne te dis pas.*

Serves 4

1 tablespoon butter

2¹/₄ lb carrots, chopped

1 cup onions, chopped

2 garlic cloves, crushed

4-in piece of fresh ginger,
peeled and finely chopped

2¹/₄ cups hot vegetable stock

1 cup heavy cream

sprig of fresh cilantro,
finely chopped (optional)

sea salt and freshly ground
black pepper

CARROT AND GINGER SOUP

Carrot also tastes great with orange—to make carrot and orange soup, omit the ginger and replace ³/₄ cup of the stock with fresh orange juice.

TIP
Store all your butter wrappers in a container in the fridge. When you are sweating vegetables, tuck the butter wrapper around them and they will sweat beautifully.

Melt the butter in a heavy-bottomed saucepan over medium heat. Add the carrot, onions, garlic, and ginger, season with salt and pepper and stir well. Cover, reduce the heat to low and leave to cook for about 15 minutes, stirring occasionally.

Stir in the hot vegetable stock and bring the soup to a boil. When the carrot is tender the soup is ready to be blended. Stir in the cream and cilantro and remove from the heat. Blend the soup in a food processor or with a hand-held immersion blender until smooth.

BAKED SPINACH, TOMATO, AND RICOTTA PASTA

This spinach, tomato, and ricotta sauce is really versatile—try using it to stuff cannelloni, or simply combine with pasta for a quicker version of this dish.

Serves 6

1¼ lb penne pasta
3 tablespoons olive oil
1 onion, thinly sliced
2 garlic cloves, finely sliced
2 x 14-oz cans chopped plum tomatoes
pinch of sugar
leaves from 2 sprigs of basil
2 tablespoons butter
10¼ oz spinach, thoroughly washed
¼ nutmeg, grated
1½ cups crumbly ricotta
1 cup grated Parmesan cheese
sea salt and freshly ground black pepper

Preheat the oven to 350°F.

Fill the largest saucepan you have with cold water and add a pinch of salt. Cover and bring to a boil. When the water is at a rolling boil, stir in the pasta and leave to cook for 3-4 minutes. (It should be just al dente because it will cook further in the oven later.) Drain and rinse under cold running water.

Make the tomato sauce by placing a saucepan over low heat. Add the oil, followed by the onion and garlic. Leave to cook for a minute, then stir in the tomatoes, sugar, and basil. Season with salt and pepper.

Meanwhile, put the butter in a frying pan and add a handful of spinach and the nutmeg. Cook the spinach, turning it over as it cooks, and add more as it wilts until all of the spinach is in the pan.

When the spinach is cooked, chop it up finely and mix with the tomato sauce and ricotta. Stir in the pasta, mix well and scoop into a large baking dish. Sprinkle the Parmesan over the pasta and cook in the oven for 15 minutes.

LEMONGRASS AND GINGER INFUSED CRÈME BRÛLÉE

If you're a fan of crème brûlée, I suggest investing in a little blowtorch. I love mine—I even use it as a weapon to scare grazers out of my kitchen!

Serves 6

4-in piece of fresh ginger, peeled and chopped
2 lemongrass stalks, chopped
⅓ cup milk
1 vanilla pod, split
1 cup heavy cream
6 eggs
⅓ cup superfine sugar (or vanilla sugar if you have it), plus extra for sprinkling

Preheat the oven to 300°F.

Put the ginger and lemongrass in a food processor and blend to a paste (alternatively grind to a paste using a mortar and pestle).

Put a saucepan over low heat and pour in the milk, vanilla pod, and cream. Stir in the ginger and lemongrass paste and heat gently until hot but not boiling.

Crack the eggs into a large mixing bowl, add the sugar, and whisk until fluffy. Slowly pour the hot cream over the egg mixture, mixing vigorously. Strain the mixture through a fine sieve into a medium shallow ovenproof dish and bake for about 40 minutes or until set.

Remove from the oven and allow to cool. Sprinkle with sugar and caramelize using a blowtorch.

CRÊPES SUZETTE

A classic desset: sweet, delicate, and lip-smacking. If
you can, make the batter the night before because it
will be much easier to work with.

Serves 4

juice and zest of
2 oranges
¾ cup superfine sugar
5 tablespoons butter
½ cup Cointreau
butter or oil,
for greasing

For the batter

1 cup all-purpose flour
2 eggs
1 cup milk
1 tablespoon melted
butter

First make the crêpe batter. Put the flour into a large
bowl and make a well in the center. Break the eggs
into the center and gradually mix in the flour. Pour
in the milk a little at a time, whisking continuously.
Put in the fridge to settle for 1-2 hours. Just before
you want to use the batter, stir in the melted butter
to help prevent the batter from sticking to the pan.

Put the orange juice and zest in a small saucepan with
the sugar and butter. Put over high heat until the
butter has melted, then reduce the heat and allow to
simmer for 10-15 minutes. At this stage the sauce
should be quite syrupy.

Preheat the oven to 300°F. Put a frying pan (or a
crêpe pan, if you have one) over medium heat and
grease with a little butter or oil. Pour a ladle
of batter into the pan, and allow to cook for
1-2 minutes, then flip it over and cook on the other
side. The crêpe should be a golden brown. Repeat with
the remaining batter to make 8 crêpes.

Fold the crêpes into quarters and transfer to an
ovenproof dish. Pour the orange syrup over the crêpes
and put in the oven for 3 minutes. Meanwhile, pour the
Cointreau into the small saucepan and heat. Once the
crêpes are warmed, pour the liqueur over the crêpes and
carefully flambé by lighting with a match. As soon as
the flames have died down, transfer to serving plates.

CHOCOLATE, ORANGE, AND CARDAMOM PANCAKES

To make flavored sugar, add a few cardamom pods, vanilla pods, lavender sprigs, or star anise to a jar of superfine sugar and leave to infuse for a couple of days.

Serves 4

For the batter

1 cup all-purpose flour, sifted
2 eggs
$2/3$ cup milk
zest and juice of 1 orange
2 tablespoons melted butter, plus extra for frying

For the sauce

8 oz good-quality dark chocolate, broken into pieces
$1/3$ cup flavored sugar, or superfine sugar
10 cardamom pods, crushed and seeds taken out (you use the seeds)
3 tablespoons heavy cream
zest and juice of $1/2$ orange

Make the pancake batter as for Crêpes Suzette (see page 45), adding the orange juice and zest with the milk, and leave in the fridge to settle.

Meanwhile, make the sauce. Put all the ingredients for the sauce into a saucepan over low heat and stir until the chocolate has melted. Set aside.

When the batter has rested for 1 hour, take it out of the fridge and give it a good whisk. Heat an 8-in nonstick frying pan and add just enough melted butter to glaze the pan. Swirl the pan to coat evenly with butter.

Preheat the oven to 300°F. Pour enough batter to cover the pan and swirl around to get an even spread. Cook for 1-2 minutes, flip over the pancake with a spatula and cook for 1 minute on the other side. Transfer to a warm plate, cover with aluminum foil and put in the oven to keep warm. Continue until you have used all of the batter.

Reheat the sauce over low heat; if it has thickened whisk in 1-2 tablespoons water. Pour the sauce over the pancakes and serve.

ITALIAN SALAD WITH PROSCIUTTO, PINE NUTS, PARMESAN, AND GOAT CHEESE CROSTINIS

This salad will only take you about five minutes to prepare. It's light and tasty, perfect as a Valentine's Day starter or a quick lunch.

Serves 2

1 small focaccia loaf, sliced

1/2 cup goat cheese

3 1/2 oz arugula salad leaves

1/2 cup pine nuts

3 tablespoons Parmesan cheese shavings

10 sun-dried tomatoes

6 slices of prosciutto

For the dressing

3 tablespoons balsamic vinegar

1/2 cup extra virgin olive oil

1/2 teaspoon Dijon mustard

1/2 garlic clove, crushed

First make the salad dressing. Put all of the ingredients into a bowl and mix well. (If you wish to store the dressing, transfer to a sterilized jar and it will keep in the fridge for 1 month.)

Preheat the oven to 350°F. Smear the goat cheese onto the focaccia slices and roast in the hot oven for about 5 minutes until toasted.

Meanwhile, put the arugula leaves, pine nuts, Parmesan shavings, and sun-dried tomatoes into 2 large serving dishes and add the salad dressing. Add 3 slices of prosciutto to each salad and serve with the goat cheese crostinis.

FILET MIGNON

Serves 2

2 filets mignons, each
about 6 oz
1 tablespoon olive oil
3 tablespoons butter
1 sprig rosemary, leaves
removed and chopped
1 garlic clove, crushed
sea salt and freshly
ground pepper

Preheat the oven to 400°F.

Take the steaks out of the fridge 30 minutes before
you're going to cook them. This will allow the meat
to relax so you get a more tender result. Season with
salt and lots of pepper.

Put an ovenproof frying or griddle pan over medium
heat and add the olive oil and butter. When the butter
has melted add the rosemary and garlic. Turn up the
heat a little and sear the steaks on both sides (about
2 minutes per side) so that they are nicely browned.
Transfer to the oven and cook for 4-5 minutes for
medium rare.

Serve with my Skinny Fries (see page 53), green beans,
grilled asparagus or buttered nutmeg spinach, and
Béarnaise Sauce (see below).

BÉARNAISE SAUCE

Serves 2

4 tablespoons white wine
vinegar
1 shallot, finely chopped
12 tablespoons
(1½ sticks) butter
3 egg yolks
1 tablespoon finely
chopped tarragon
sea salt and freshly
ground black pepper

Put the vinegar, shallot, and 4 tablespoons of water
in a saucepan over medium heat to simmer for 3 minutes
or until reduced by one-third. Remove from the heat.

Melt the butter in a separate pan.

Put the egg yolks into a food-processor and blend.
Slowly pour the melted butter into the egg yolks,
continuing to process, until the mixture is creamy and
thick. Stir in the shallots and tarragon and season
with salt and pepper.

Serve warm. If the sauce separates add a cube of ice
and whisk vigorously.

THE PERFECT SKINNY FRIES

No, unfortunately they won't make you skinny, but they are so good, especially when dipped in béarnaise sauce, that you won't care. You can, of course, deep-fry these, but I don't own a deep fryer so I make them in a shallow pan. Although the recipe suggests using fresh rosemary, you could use 1 tablespoon of the dried herb instead. Whenever I'm in New York I buy a can of dried rosemary from Dean and Deluca, which sells wonderful dried herbs and spices. So go on, dip and enjoy and forget about those skinny jeans for just one evening.

Makes enough for 2 greedy skinny fry lovers

canola or sunflower oil, for frying

4 large baking potatoes, cut into long skinny fries (leave the skin on because it adds flavor and is a good source of fiber)

1 tablespoon olive oil

2 sprigs of rosemary, leaves removed and finely chopped

sea salt and freshly ground black pepper

Preheat the oven to 400°F.

Put a frying pan on the stove and fill two-thirds full with oil. Turn the heat up as far as it will go.

Dab the raw potato with paper towels to remove any excess moisture. When the oil is hot, use a slotted spoon to place a batch of fries into the oil. They should take 4-5 minutes to cook. Work in as many batches as you need to cook all the fries.

Remove from the oil and toss in olive oil, rosemary, and salt and pepper. Cook in the oven for 5 minutes.

RED VELVET CUPCAKES

A clever little tip is to crumble one of your un-iced cupcakes into fine crumbs and sprinkle on top of the icing to make a pretty decoration.

Makes 24 cupcakes

2 tablespoons cocoa powder

3 tablespoons red food coloring

1 teaspoon vanilla extract

8 tablespoons (1 stick) butter, softened

1 cup superfine sugar

4 egg yolks

1 cup buttermilk

2 cups all-purpose flour, sifted

1 teaspoon baking powder

For the icing

12 tablespoons (1½ sticks) butter

³/₄ cup confectioners' sugar

1 teaspoon vanilla extract

Preheat the oven to 350°F. Line two 12-hole cupcake pans with paper baking cups and set aside.

Put the cocoa, food coloring, and vanilla extract in a small bowl and mix well. Put the butter and sugar in a large bowl and use a hand mixer to beat them together. Add the yolks and beat for 1 more minute. Add in the cocoa mixture and continue to mix for another minute. Slowly mix in the buttermilk, followed by the flour and baking powder.

Fill each paper cup with 3 tablespoons of the mixture and bake for about 15 minutes or until a toothpick inserted in the center comes out clean. Allow to cool a little in the pans then transfer to a wire rack for 15 minutes before icing.

Make the icing by beating together the butter, confectioners' sugar, and vanilla extract to give a thick, creamy consistency. Either put the icing in a piping bag or dip a spoon in hot water and smear the icing on the cupcakes. Decorate with cake crumbs.

Makes 24 macaroons

For the shells

1 cup ground almonds

1 cup confectioners' sugar

1/3 cup egg white (about 3 extra large eggs)

1/3 cup superfine sugar

1/2 teaspoon rosewater essence

liquid red food coloring

For the filling

1/3 cup heavy cream

3 1/2 oz white chocolate, cut into small pieces

2 teaspoons butter, diced

1 tablespoon rosewater essence

ROSEWATER MACAROONS

Macaroons can be a bit tricky to make, but if you are a keen baker you should definitely try them. Just ensure you make them in a cool area, since the shells can melt.

Preheat the oven to 250°F. Line two medium baking sheets with parchment paper or prepare nonstick baking mats.

First make the macaroon shells. Sift the ground almonds and confectioners' sugar together into a large bowl and set aside. Beat the egg white using an electric mixer on high speed until foamy, then gradually add the superfine sugar and rosewater essence. Continue beating the egg white until it forms glossy stiff peaks. Add the liquid coloring a drop at a time, stirring well after each addition, until the desired color is achieved.

Mix the egg white into the ground almond mixture and continue to mix the egg white with the dry ingredients until well combined. The mixture should be thick, glossy, and well-blended and look like a thick cake batter.

Next is the fun part! Spoon the mixture into a piping bag fitted with a plain 1/2 in nozzle. Pipe the mixture onto the lined baking sheets or mats, making macaroons about 1in across and spacing them about 1in apart. Tap the trays on the work surface a couple of times to flatten the macaroons and remove any air bubbles. Leave the shells, uncovered, at room temperature for about 1 hour or until you can touch the shells without them sticking to your fingers.

Meanwhile, make the filling. Put the heavy cream into a saucepan over low heat. When it comes to a boil, remove from the heat and stir in the white chocolate pieces. Stir the mixture until the chocolate is completely melted. Stir in the butter and rosewater essence and mix until well combined. Chill the filling for at least 1 hour until firm.

Cook the macaroons for about 15 minutes. Transfer the macaroons to wire racks to cool (you may need to use a knife to lift the macaroons). When they are completely cool, sandwich two shells together with the chocolate filling. Store in an airtight container in the fridge.

RHUBARB AND GINGER JAM

A handy tip is to use the top of a teaspoon to peel fresh ginger. It's easier to get around the knobbly bits and it's so much faster than a peeler.

Cut the rhubarb into 2-in pieces and put into a large bowl with the sugar, fresh ginger, crystallized ginger, and lemon zest and juice. Mix well, cover, and set aside for 3 hours or overnight so that the flavors from the ginger and lemon infuse into the rhubarb.

Put the rhubarb and all the juices into a large, heavy-bottomed saucepan and put over medium heat. Stir until the sugar has completely dissolved and bring to a boil. Continue to cook for about 15 minutes until the rhubarb is really tender and has reached setting point (see Tip, right).

Remove the pan from the heat and leave to one side for 2-3 minutes before pouring into sterilized jars. The jam will keep in the fridge for 1 month.

Makes 4 x 16-oz jars

$2\frac{1}{4}$ lb trimmed rhubarb
$2\frac{1}{4}$ lb granulated sugar
4-in piece of fresh ginger, peeled and grated
3 oz crystallized ginger, finely chopped
zest and juice of 1 lemon

TIP

To test if the jam has reached setting point, drop a spoonful onto a cold saucer. Leave for 30 seconds, then gently push it with the tip of your finger. If the jam wrinkles, setting point has been reached. If not, continue to cook for an additional 1–2 minutes and test again.

RHUBARB AND HAZELNUT CRUMBLE

Individual crumbles served in china cups are perfect
for a dinner party. They look so decadent on a saucer
with a spoonfull of heavy cream.

Serves 6

1 lb 12 oz rhubarb
1/3 cup superfine sugar
1/4 cup water
1/2 cup crystallized
ginger, chopped
heavy cream, to serve

For the crumble

8 tablespoons (1 stick)
butter, chilled and cut
into cubes
3/4 cup all-purpose flour
3/4 cup hazelnuts,
roughly chopped
1/2 cup brown sugar

Preheat the oven to 350°F.

Cut the rhubarb into 4-in pieces and toss in a bowl
with the sugar. Pour into a roasting pan with the
water and cook in the oven for 10 minutes. Fill
an ovenproof dish about 1 1/2 in deep with the rhubarb.

To make the crumble, rub the butter into the flour,
hazelnuts, and sugar. Sprinkle the mixture over the
rhubarb and bake in the oven for 35-45 minutes. Spoon
into 6 china cups and serve with heavy cream.

RHUBARB AND VANILLA UPSIDE DOWN CAKE

This also works well made with apples in place of the rhubarb. Simply peel, core, and slice your apples into thickish slices and make as below.

Serves 8-10

13 tablespoons butter, softened

½ cup light brown sugar

1 lb rhubarb

3 eggs, separated

½ cup superfine sugar

1½ cups all-purpose flour, sifted

2 teaspoons baking powder

⅓ cup milk

1 teaspoon vanilla extract

lightly whipped cream, to serve

Preheat the oven to 350°F.

Melt 6 tablespoons of the butter in a 12in nonstick ovenproof pan and swirl it around to coat the whole pan. Stir in the light brown sugar and cook, stirring, for 2 minutes until the sugar begins to melt. Remove from the heat.

Cut the rhubarb into 4-in pieces and place on top of the sugar mixture in the pan.

Whisk the eggs whites until stiff and gradually beat in half the superfine sugar.

Put the remaining butter and superfine sugar into a food processor and beat until light and fluffy. Beat in the egg yolks one at a time. Start to add the flour and baking powder a little at a time, followed by the milk and vanilla extract, mixing until well blended and using a spatula to scrape the mixture from the sides of the bowl so that it is completely mixed in.

Fold in the egg whites. I like to mix in the first spoonful of egg whites and combine before folding in the remainder. Spoon the batter on top of the rhubarb in the pan and smooth it out evenly with the back of a spoon. Bake in the oven for 40 minutes. Test the cake by inserting a skewer into the center of the cake; if it comes out clean the cake is cooked.

Leave the cake to cool in the pan for 10 minutes, then flip it on to a plate and lift off the pan. Serve with lightly whipped cream.

Mint and Chocolate
Cupcakes

Mini Guinness

MARCH

ST. PATRICK'S DAY

When I was a kid I loved St. Patrick's Day. The day would start with a breakfast of crispy bacon, potato cakes, and soda bread, then off to mass. After church, Mum got the stew started and we made brooches for the parade: Irish flags or a harp. The biggest and best float (hands up if you remember) was the bubble gum float. Pretty girls would throw bucket-loads of bubble gum at the screaming, scrambling kids.

By the time the parade was over I'd be freezing, more often than not soaked to the bone, but as happy as a clam because my pockets were full of bubble gum. Back home the smell of Beef and Guinness Stew would hit us as soon as the front door opened. My mum made the best stew in Ireland, everyone's mum did. She'd cut the carrots into big chunks and let the whole thing cook for at least a couple of hours. She'd serve it with creamy champ, with a blob of butter on top and colcannon.

I'm going to make a confession here: as a kid I never liked Cabbage and Bacon soup, our traditional St. Patrick's Day starter. Like all good things it took a while to grow on me. Now, I love it. I've included it it in this chapter, a mixture of Mum's recipe and my own.

CABBAGE AND BACON SOUP

When NBC's Today Show came to Ireland I was very proud to be asked to cook something traditionally Irish with a twist for the show. We filmed in a lovely pub in Galway and this is what I cooked for Matt Lauer and Hoda Kotb.

Serves 6

4 tablespoons butter

12 bacon slices or pancetta, diced

2 small potatoes, peeled and diced

2 garlic cloves, crushed

$2/3$ cup onions, chopped

$1^1/4$ cups hot chicken or vegetable stock

2 teaspoons dried oregano

$1^1/4$ cups tomatoes, chopped

$4^1/4$ cups cabbage, shredded

sea salt and freshly ground black pepper

Put a heavy-bottomed saucepan over medium heat. Add the butter, and when it has melted stir in the bacon, potatoes, garlic, and onions. Cover and cook for 10 minutes.

Add the stock, oregano, and tomatoes and bring to a boil. Add in the cabbage, reduce the heat, and cook for about 5 minutes until all the vegetables are tender. Season to taste with salt and pepper and serve with chunks of buttered bread.

CHEDDAR CHEESE SOUP SCONES

I love matching up little scones with soups; try using different flavors to match the soup that you are serving.

Makes 8 Scones

$1^3/_4$ cups all-purpose flour

1 teaspoon baking powder

pinch of sea salt

4 tablespoons butter

1 cup mature Cheddar cheese, grated

1 teaspoon chopped thyme leaves

$^1/_2$ cup milk

oil, for greasing

Preheat the oven to 400°F.

Sift the flour, baking powder, and sea salt into a bowl. Rub the butter into the flour mixture until it resembles fine breadcrumbs. Stir in two-thirds of the grated cheese, followed by the thyme. Gradually pour in enough of the milk to make a soft dough.

Roll out the dough on a lightly floured surface to about $^1/_2$ in thick and use a pastry cutter or upturned glass to cut circles. Transfer the scones to a greased baking sheet and sprinkle the remaining cheese over the scones. Bake in the oven for 12-15 minutes, then transfer to a wire cooling rack for 5 minutes.

65

IRISH CHEESE SOUFFLÉS

The secret to making lovely, lofty soufflés is to not be tempted to open the oven before they are ready and to serve them straight from the oven.

Makes 4 soufflés

2 tablespoons butter, plus extra for greasing

2 tablespoons all-purpose flour

1 cup milk, warmed

1 cup Coolea cheese, finely grated (this is an Irish cheese—if you cannot find it, use a cheese like Gouda instead)

$1/2$ teaspoon ground nutmeg

4 large eggs, separated

sea salt and freshly ground black pepper

Preheat the oven to 400°F. Butter 4 individual ramekins.

Put the butter in a saucepan over low heat. When it has melted, stir in the flour and continue to stir until a roux forms. Whisk in the milk a little at a time until you have a creamy sauce.

Stir in the cheese and nutmeg and mix well. Beat in the egg yolks, one at a time, then remove the saucepan from the heat and continue to stir for a few minutes. Season with salt and pepper.

Whisk the egg whites to stiff peaks, then fold them into the cheese mixture. Fill the ramekins with the soufflé mix and immediately bake in the oven for 25 minutes. Be careful not to open the oven door for the first 20 minutes, or the soufflés will flop.

POTATO CAKES

You can make this the night before and then just reheat in the oven the next day. Sometimes I add grated Cheddar cheese or finely chopped pancetta to the potato mix.

Makes 6 potato cakes

$2^1/_4$ lb potatoes, peeled
$^1/_2$ cup crème fraîche
1 egg yolk
1 teaspoon Dijon mustard
2 tablespoons chopped scallions, steamed shredded cabbage, or steamed leeks
2 tablespoons all-purpose flour
2 tablespoons butter
sea salt and freshly ground black pepper

Cook the potatoes in a large saucepan of boiling salted water until tender. Drain, transfer to a bowl, and mash with a potato masher.

While the potatoes are still hot mix in the crème fraîche, egg yolk, mustard, and salt and pepper. Mix in the scallions, cabbage, or leeks.

Add 1 tablespoon of the flour to the mixture to help make the consistency suitable for rolling out and sprinkle the remaining flour on your work surface. Roll the potato mixture out to 2 in thick using a rolling pin and cut it into circles using a 4-in cookie or biscuit cutter.

Melt the butter in a frying pan and fry the potato cakes on both sides until golden brown.

HONEY-GLAZED HAM
STUFFED WITH APPLE

If you can't get your hands on a leg of pork, then use a piece of smoked or unsmoked ham.

Serves 8

3 lb boneless or semiboneless fully cooked ham (if the rind is on, make sure you score it)
salt and pepper

For the glaze

4 tablespoons butter
2 small cooking apples, peeled, cored and chopped
1 onion, finely chopped
2-in piece of fresh ginger, peeled and grated
1/2 cup brown sugar
1/2 teaspoon chili powder
4 cloves
1/2 cup cider vinegar
sea salt and freshly ground black pepper

Preheat the oven to 375°F.

First make the glaze. Put the butter in a saucepan over medium heat. When the butter has melted stir in the apples, onion, and ginger, season with salt and pepper, and cook for 3 minutes. Add the sugar, chili powder, and cloves, stir well, cover and cook for 3 minutes.

Pour in the vinegar, bring to a boil, and simmer for about 20 minutes. Use the back of a wooden spoon to mash up the apples so the mixture is nice and thick. At this stage you can transfer the mixture to a sterilized jar and it will keep for up to 3 months.

Remove the ham from of the fridge and cover it with the spiced apple. Cook in the oven for 1 hour 40 minutes, basting every 20 minutes.

GUINNESS AND BEEF STEW

The longer and the lower temperature that you cook this stew, the better the flavor. I recommend that you make it the day before you plan to eat it because the flavors concentrate much more.

Serves 8

2 tablespoons butter
14 bacon slices, chopped
10$\frac{1}{2}$ oz shallots, left whole
2$\frac{1}{4}$ lb stewing beef, cubed
14 oz mixed wild mushrooms
1 quart Guinness
1 bouquet garni
sea salt and freshly ground black pepper

Preheat the oven to 325°F.

Put the butter in a frying pan over medium heat. When the butter has melted add the bacon, followed by the shallots. Cook until golden brown and transfer to a large baking dish.

Add the beef to the frying pan, season with salt and pepper and cook until browned all over. Transfer to the baking dish.

Add the mushrooms to the pan and cook for 2 minutes. Season to taste and transfer to the baking dish.

Return the frying pan to the stove over medium heat and use a whisk to scrape off all the bits stuck to the bottom of the pan (this is where the flavor is). Pour in the Guinness and continue to whisk for another minute to deglaze the pan. Pour the Guinness and pan juices over the beef and vegetables in the baking dish. Add the bouquet garni, cover the baking dish and cook in the oven for 2 hours.

Check the seasoning, remove the bouquet garni, and serve with roasted potatoes.

MINT AND CHOCOLATE CUPCAKES

These are just so cute! I box them up and give them to my friends on St. Patrick's Day. We can't make enough of these in my bakery on Paddy's Day.

Makes 18 cupcakes

1¾ cups self-rising flour

1 teaspoon baking powder

4 tablespoons cocoa powder

2 sticks unsalted butter

1¼ cups superfine sugar

4 eggs

1 teaspoon mint extract

3½ oz dark chocolate chips

For the decoration

2¼ cups confectioners' sugar, sifted

1 teaspoon mint extract

1 stick unsalted butter, softened

green food coloring

3½ oz dark chocolate chips

Preheat the oven to 350°F. Line an 18-hole cupcake pan with paper baking cups.

Sift the flour, baking powder, and cocoa into a bowl.

Put the butter and sugar into another bowl and use an electric whisk to beat them together until light and fluffy. Add the eggs one at a time, beating the mixture as you go, then stir in the mint extract and chocolate chips. Fold in the flour mixture and mix well.

Spoon the cake mixture into the cups and bake in the oven for about 20 minutes or until a toothpick inserted into the center comes out clean.

Meanwhile, make the icing. Whisk together the confectioners' sugar, mint extract, and butter. Stir in just enough food coloring to turn the icing mint green. Ice the cooled cakes and decorate the tops with chocolate chips.

IRISH COFFEE

Ok, I'm an Irish gal and a chef, so if I can't make a
good Irish Coffee, well... This traditional Irish tipple
is too good to be served just once a year on St.
Patrick's Day—they are a lovely way to finish a dinner
party and are a great pick-me-up on a cold and gloomy
winter evening.

Makes 1

2 tablespoons Irish
whiskey
2 teaspoons brown sugar
½ cup good-quality
strong coffee
cream

Carefully warm a glass. Add the Irish whiskey to the
warmed glass and stir in the sugar.

Pour in the coffee and, using the back of a spoon,
pour the cream onto the surface of the coffee.

MINI GUINNESS

This mousse is light and fluffy yet rich thanks to the good quality chocolate. I suggest that you use chocolate that has 70 percent cocoa solids.

Makes 12 shot glasses

7 oz good-quality chocolate

½ cup heavy cream

1 teaspoon superfine sugar

4 eggs, separated

½ cup good-quality strong espresso coffee, cold

To serve

1 cup whipped heavy cream

grated chocolate or chocolate-coated coffee beans

Break the chocolate into a heatproof bowl suspended over a saucepan of simmering water. Melt the chocolate, stirring often to make sure that no lumps form.

Remove the bowl from the heat and stir in the cream, sugar, egg yolks, and coffee.

In a clean bowl whisk the eggs whites until stiff peaks form. Fold the egg whites into the chocolate mixture. Pour the chocolate mixture into individual shot glasses and put in the fridge for 1 hour or until they are set.

Before serving top with whipped heavy cream and decorate with a grating of chocolate or chocolate-coated coffee beans.

MOTHER'S DAY

On Mother's Day (which is celebrated in March in Ireland) I like to make my mum a beautiful afternoon tea. After all it was from her I learned my love of baking. When I was little she would bake every Saturday morning for the week ahead, filling the house with a delicious buttery, vanilla smell. I'd watch from my stool, desperate to have my turn on the hand-held blender or to turn the dial on the Kenwood mixer.

One year I did a Mother's Day tea for friends who were young mums. I invested in a mini cupcake stand and spent a heavenly morning decorating the cakes with sugar flowers and butterfly decorations. You can buy amazing cupcake decorations in most good food stores. I used my prettiest china and linen and decorated the table with small jam jars of wildflowers. You can buy beautiful little doilies that are perfect for large cakes or tarts and look gorgeous. It was a real treat but also felt a bit naughty and decadent.

At Clodagh's Bakery we do a Mothering Sunday high tea. Our famous Buttermilk Scones are very popular, so too is my mum's favorite Lemon Drizzle cake. Just in case you fancy impressing your mother with your home baking, I've included recipes from The Bakery in this chapter. The main thing is not where you take your mother or the cakes, it's spending time together and making her feel precious and appreciated.

EGG SALAD MINI ROLLS

An afternoon classic. The key is not to overcook the eggs.
I find 6 minutes in boiling water cooks them perfectly.

Makes 6

3 eggs at room
temperature
½ tablespoon butter
1 tablespoon mayonnaise
3 chives, finely sliced
6 mini rolls
sea salt and freshly
ground black pepper

Put a saucepan of cold water over medium heat and
bring to a boil. When the water is boiling carefully
add the eggs and simmer for 6 minutes. Drain the eggs
and cool under cold running water. Remove the shells.

Mash the eggs together with the butter, mayonnaise,
chives, and season with salt and pepper.

Cut the mini rolls in half, spoon the egg salad onto
the bottom halves and replace the top halves.

ROAST BEEF AND HORSERADISH MINI ROLLS

Perfect for leftover roast beef. When I cook roast beef
at home halfway through dinner I'm already planning this
sandwich for the following day.

Makes 12

1 cup crème fraîche
3 tablespoons
horseradish, grated
½ teaspoon Dijon
mustard
juice of ½ lemon
12 mini rolls
24 arugula leaves
6 thin slices of roast
beef, halved
sea salt and freshly
ground black pepper

Put the crème fraîche, horseradish, mustard, and lemon
juice in a bowl, season with salt and pepper, and
mix well.

Cut the mini rolls in half. Put 2 arugula leaves on
the bottom halves. Top with a piece of beef and add
a dollop of the horseradish cream. Replace the top
halves of the rolls.

CUCUMBER, SALMON, AND CREAM CHEESE SANDWICHES

Use good organic or wild smoked salmon for this. I'm lucky to live in Ireland where we have some of the world's best fish smokers.

Makes 32 small rectangular sandwiches

8 slices of wholegrain bread

½ cup cream cheese, softened

7 oz smoked salmon

½ cucumber, thinly sliced

sea salt and freshly ground black pepper

Smear the bread with cream cheese.

Layer a slice of smoked salmon and a few slices of cucumber on 4 slices of the bread and season with salt and pepper. Sandwich together with the remaining slices of bread.

Use a serrated knife to cut off the crusts. Cut each sandwich diagonally into quarters.

MINI JAM TARTS

You may not use all the jam but it's better to have 2 jars just in case, because you don't want any tarts going unfilled! You can freeze the uncooked pastry cases.

For the pastry

1¾ cups all-purpose flour, plus extra for dusting

1 stick unsalted butter, chilled and diced, plus extra for greasing

1 teaspoon superfine sugar

1 egg yolk

2 tablespoons cold water

For the filling

2 jars of good quality strawberry or raspberry jam

Preheat the oven to 350°F. Lightly grease and dust two 12-hole mini tart baking sheets.

To make the pastry, sift the flour into a large bowl and rub in the butter with your fingertips (if you prefer, you can blend the butter and flour together in a food processor). The mixture should resemble fine breadcrumbs. Mix in the sugar.

Mix in the yolk, add the water, and knead the mixture until it forms a dough. Wrap it in plastic wrap and put in the fridge to chill for 30 minutes.

Roll out the dough on a lightly floured surface to about ¼-in thick and cut out 24 small circles with a cookie cutter. Put the pastry circles over each hole of the tart sheet and gently push the pastry into the hole. Use a fork to pierce a few holes in each tart case. Bake in the oven for 5 minutes, remove, and fill with the jam. Return to the oven for an additional 10 minutes.

Allow the tarts to cool in the baking sheets for 5 minutes, then remove to a wire rack to cool completely before serving.

Makes 24 scones

7$\frac{1}{4}$ cups self-rising flour,
  plus extra for dusting
1 teaspoon baking powder
$\frac{1}{2}$ cup superfine sugar
2$\frac{1}{4}$ cups buttermilk or whole
  milk, plus extra for glazing
2$\frac{2}{3}$ cups butter, softened
2 tablespoons golden raisins

OUR FAMED BUTTERMILK SCONES

Have light hands with the dough and don't over work it
or you won't get a light, fluffy scone. You can
substitute the raisins for cranberries or blueberries.

Preheat the oven to 475°F. Lightly dust two baking sheets.

Sift the flour and the baking powder into a large mixing
bowl and mix in the sugar. Make a well in the center and
slowly pour in the buttermilk or milk, using your other
hand to mix the milk into the flour as you pour. Stir in the
golden raisins.

Using floured hands, bring the dough together and roll it out
to about 1-in thick. Use a biscuit cutter to cut out the
scones and put onto the baking sheets.

Brush with a little milk and bake in the oven for 5 minutes.
Reduce the temperature to 325°F and cook for an additional
20 minutes.

COFFEE, WALNUT, AND CARDAMOM CAKE

I love coffee cake in the afternoon with freshly brewed tea—add cardamom to the mix and I'm in afternoon heaven. If you are not as big a fan of cardamom as I am, just omit it.

Serves 8-10

1³/₄ sticks butter at room temperature

1 cup superfine sugar

3 eggs

1²/₃ cups self-rising flour

1 teaspoon baking powder

seeds from 10 cardamom pods, crushed

3 tablespoons espresso coffee

½ cup walnuts, finely chopped

For the icing

2½ cups confectioners' sugar

1³/₄ sticks butter

½ cup espresso coffee

1 teaspoon cardamom seeds, crushed

6 walnuts, halved

Preheat the oven to 350°F. Grease and line the base and sides of a 8-9-in round cake pan.

Put the butter in a large mixing bowl with the sugar and beat together with a whisk until light and fluffy.

Slowly beat in the eggs, one at a time. When the eggs are fully incorporated, fold in the flour, baking powder, cardamom seeds, coffee, and walnuts.

Pour the cake mixture into the pan and tap the sides to release any air bubbles. Bake in the oven for 35-40 minutes or until the cake is lightly golden brown. Check by inserting a skewer into the middle of the cake; if it comes out clean the cake is cooked.

Meanwhile, make the icing. Whisk together the confectioners' sugar, butter, coffee, and cardamom seeds until you get a light and fluffy icing.

Leave the cooked cake to cool for 10 minutes in the pan, then remove to cool completely on a wire rack. Cut horizontally through the center of the cake.

Spread half of the icing on the top of the bottom half of the cake. Place the top half in position and cover with the remaining icing. Decorate the top with the halved walnuts.

Roasted
Rosemary
and Garlic-
Infused Leg
of Lamb

Lemon
Meringue
Pie

APRIL

NEW YORK

I got a call to appear and give a cooking demonstration on
the Rachael Ray Show in New York. They also wanted to show
a clip of my series *Clodagh's Irish Food Trails*, which was
about to air on PBS in America. I was thrilled. Rachel Ray
is massively popular—a celebrity chef, author, and television
personality—and it was a great opportunity to promote the
show. No worries.

It was only when I got out of the car on Madison Avenue that
I realized just how big Rachael Ray is. Her name is emblazoned
across the front of the building where the show is shot. People
were lining up around the block to be in the studio audience.
I thought my heart was going to leap out of my chest.

Rachael completely put me at ease, making me feel like I was
in her kitchen, just sharing tips with a fellow cook. I cooked
my Roasted Rosemary and Garlic-Infused Leg of Lamb, followed
by Coffee Chocolate Mousses, with a white chocolate froth on
top. You guessed it, like a glass of Guinness! I was keen for
the presentation to reflect my vintage style. Her fantastic
stylists found beautiful fifties martini glasses to serve the
mousse in. I was really pleased with the result. The glasses
gave the dessert a real elegance. I still can't believe it all
happened. I have to watch the recording to remind myself it
really did.

ASPARAGUS, MINT, AND RICOTTA TARTLETS

Super simple to make and so tasty. Use asparagus in the recipe while it's in season, but you can substitute with lots of other vegetables when it isn't, such as tomatoes or zucchini.

Makes 4

1 sheet of ready-rolled all-butter puff pastry

8 oz ricotta

3/4 cup Parmesan cheese, finely grated

finely grated rind of 1 lemon

8 asparagus spears

olive oil, for brushing

sea salt and freshly ground black pepper

mint leaves, to serve

Preheat the oven to 400°F. Line a baking sheet with nonstick parchment paper.

Cut out four rectangles, each 5 × 2 1/2 in, from the pastry sheet and place them on the baking sheet. Score a 1/2 in border on each rectangle.

Put the ricotta, Parmesan, lemon rind, salt, and pepper into a bowl and stir to combine. Spoon the mixture on to the pastry and top each tart with two asparagus spears. Brush the pastry borders with oil and cook in the oven for 12-15 minutes or until the pastry is puffed and golden.

Serve with a couple of mint leaves on top.

GOOD FRIDAY FISH—ROASTED HAKE WITH MINTED HOLLANDAISE SAUCE

I eat a lot of fish, being the granddaughter and niece of fishermen and also making two TV series and writing a cookbook on the subject. You are going to love my foolproof recipe for hollandaise sauce—I promise you it won't split! You can substitute the mint for basil, tarragon, or any herb you like.

Serves 2

2 fillets of hake
3 tablespoons olive oil, plus extra for tossing
10 asparagus spears
sea salt and freshly ground black pepper

For the hollandaise sauce

1³/₄ sticks butter
5 egg yolks
juice of 1 lemon
leaves from sprig of mint, finely chopped

Preheat the oven to 350°F.

Season the hake on both sides with salt and pepper. Put an ovenproof pan over medium heat and pour in the olive oil. When the oil is hot add the fish, skin side down, and sear for 2 minutes. Turn over and sear the other side for 2 minutes before placing in the oven for 10 minutes.

Meanwhile, make the hollandaise sauce. Heat the butter in a saucepan over low heat until melted. Pour the egg yolks and lemon juice into a food processor. Set the food processor to medium speed and slowly pour in the melted butter until all the butter is well blended with the egg yolks and the sauce is thickened.

Toss the asparagus in a little olive oil, season with salt and pepper, and roast in the oven for 8-10 minutes. Serve with new potatoes scattered with mint leaves.

ROASTED ROSEMARY AND GARLIC-INFUSED LEG OF LAMB

I made this wonderful Easter Sunday lunch when I was a guest on the Rachel Ray Show in the US. It was so exciting to have been asked on the show, the energy from everyone working behind the scenes was incredible!

Serves 6

4½ lb leg of spring lamb
small bunch of rosemary
3 garlic cloves, sliced
olive oil
sea salt and freshly ground black pepper

Take the lamb out of the fridge 30 minutes before you intend to cook it. This will allow the meat to relax, so that it will be more tender when it is cooked.

Preheat the oven to 400°F.

Put the lamb in a roasting pan and score the fat, then make several deep incisions across the top with a sharp knife. Push small pieces of rosemary, each about 2 in long, and a slice of garlic into each incision. Rub a small amount of olive oil over the skin and season with salt and pepper.

Roast the lamb for 20 minutes, then reduce the temperature to 350°F and cook for an additional 1 hour for rare, 1¼ hours for medium, and 1½ hours for well done.

When the lamb is cooked remove it from the pan, cover it with a tent of aluminum foil, and allow to rest for 15 minutes before carving.

THE ULTIMATE GRAVY

This is a gravy recipe I use for most of my roasts.
I vary the wine and cream depending on how rich or light
I want the gravy to be to match the piece of meat. Make
it your own by adding different herbs or wines.

Serves 6

1/2 cup red wine (optional)

2 1/2 cups chicken stock

2 garlic cloves, left whole

leaves from 1 sprig of rosemary, finely chopped

3 tablespoons butter

1/2 cup flour

1/2 cup heavy cream (optional)

sea salt and freshly ground black pepper

When you have taken the meat out of the roasting pan, put the pan over medium heat. If you are using red wine (I highly recommend it) add it to the pan and use a whisk mix it with the juices. Leave to simmer for 3 minutes to allow the alcohol to evaporate.

Add the stock, cloves, and rosemary and bring to a boil. Whisk in the butter and flour to thicken the gravy slightly. Pour in the cream (optional, but adds a lovely richness).

Taste and allow to bubble up until the flavor is concentrated enough. Season with salt and pepper and pour through a sieve into your gravy boat.

ZIPPY FRESH MINT SAUCE

5 tablespoons finely chopped fresh mint

3 tablespoons white wine vinegar

2 teaspoons superfine sugar

1 tablespoon hot water

Put all of the ingredeints into a bowl and whisk well. You have mint sauce—simple!

Serves 10

21 oz spinach
olive oil, for frying
1½ cups arborio rice
1 onion, finely chopped
8 tablespoons freshly grated
Parmesan cheese
3 eggs, lightly beaten
butter, for greasing
sea salt and freshly ground
black pepper
⅔ cup breadcrumbs

ITALIAN EASTER BAKED SPINACH AND RICE

When I lived in Turin in Northern Italy, we used to eat this traditional savory cake at Easter time. It's a great way to use up leftover risotto rice. Serve with a big green salad to add a little lightness.

Preheat the oven to 350°F.

Prepare the spinach by removing and discarding the stems and rinsing the leaves in cold water. Drain well. Heat a drop of olive oil in a frying pan over medium heat and cook the spinach until soft. Remove from the pan and chop finely.

Cook the rice according to the package instructions until al dente, then drain well. Meanwhile, place the pan used for the spinach back over the heat and add a drop of olive oil followed by the onion and cook until soft. In a large bowl mix together the spinach, onion, rice, 5 tablespoons of the Parmesan, and the eggs, and season wth salt and pepper .

Grease a medium round cake pan with butter and press the rice and spinach mixture into the pan. Sprinkle the breadcrumbs on top followed by the remaining Parmesan. Cook in the oven for 35–40 minutes or until golden.

Serves 6

For the pastry

1½ cups all-purpose flour

7 tablespoons cold butter, diced

1 tablespoon confectioners' sugar

1 egg yolk

For the filling

1 tablespoon cornstarch

juice and zest of 2 large lemons

½ cup superfine sugar

4 tablespoons butter, diced

3 egg yolks and 1 whole egg

For the meringue

4 egg whites

1 cup superfine sugar

1 teaspoon cornstarch

LEMON MERINGUE PIE

I'm not sure I've ever met anyone who doesn't like Lemon
Meringue Pie. To save time, buy a jar of lemon curd
instead of making the filling, or just mash up some
meringues and fold-in lemon curd with whipped cream.

Preheat the oven to 350°F.

First make the pastry. Put the flour, butter, confectioners' sugar, egg yolk, and 1 tablespoon cold water into a food processor and mix until combined. Place the dough onto a lightly floured surface, gather it together until smooth, then roll out and line a 9 × 1 in loose-bottomed fluted tart pan. Trim the edges and press the pastry into the flutes. Prick the base with a fork, line with aluminum foil, and chill for 1 hour.

Pour baking beans on top of the foil and blind bake the pastry for 15 minutes. Remove and allow to cool.

To prepare the filling, mix together the cornstarch, lemon zest, juice, and sugar in a medium-sized saucepan. Continue to cook over medium heat, stirring constantly, until thickened. Remove from the heat and whisk in the butter. Beat together the egg yolks (save the whites for the meringue) and the whole egg, stir into the pan, and return to medium heat. Keep stirring vigorously for a few minutes

until the mixture thickens again. Remove from the heat and set aside.

To make the meringue, put the egg whites in a large bowl, whisk to soft peaks, then add half the sugar, a spoonful at a time, whisking after each addition. Whisk in the cornstarch; add the rest of the sugar and whisk until smooth and thick.

Reheat the filling and pour it into the pastry case. Immediately put spoonfuls of meringue around the edge of the filling (if you start in the middle the meringue may sink), then spread it so it just touches the pastry. Pile the rest of the meringue into the center, spreading so it touches the surface of the hot filling (and starts to cook), then swirl using a knife to form soft peaks. Return to the oven for 18-20 minutes until the meringue is crisp and slightly colored.

Allow the pie to sit in the pan for 30 minutes, then remove and leave to cool for at least another 30-60 minutes before slicing.

Makes 12

oil, for greasing

1 cup milk

1 pack (.25 oz) active dry yeast

$^2/_3$ cup superfine sugar

$2^1/_2$ cups all-purpose flour

2 cups bread flour

$^2/_3$ cup raisins

2 tablespoons candied lemon peel, cut into 2-in pieces

2 tablespoons candied orange peel, cut into 2-in pieces

$^1/_2$ teaspoon cinnamon

$^1/_4$ teaspoon ground nutmeg

pinch of salt

4 tablespoons butter, melted

2 large eggs plus 1 yolk

1 cup confectioners' sugar

$^1/_2$ teaspoon vanilla extract

HOT CROSS BUNS

I always used to think hot cross buns were difficult to make, and avoided baking them for years. When I finally gave them a try one Easter, I realized they are really easy to make. They will keep for about 4 days in an airtight container but if they do go a little hard, toast them and spread with ample amounts of butter.

Preheat the oven to 475°F. Coat a large bowl with oil and set aside. Line a large baking sheet with parchment paper.

To make the dough, whisk together half the milk, the yeast, and 1 teaspoon of the sugar in a small bowl and leave to stand until frothy. Combine the flours, remaining sugar, raisins, candied peels, spices, and salt in the bowl of a standing mixer fitted with a dough hook and mix on low speed until combined (alternatively add the ingredients to a large bowl and combine by hand). Add the butter, 2 eggs, and the yeast mixture and continue to mix for about 3 minutes or until a sticky dough forms.

Transfer the dough to a lightly floured surface and knead by hand for about 5 minutes until smooth. (If you have combined the dough by hand increase the kneading time to 10 minutes.) Form the dough into a ball, place it in the prepared bowl, and turn to coat all sides with oil. Cover with a clean, damp kitchen towel and leave to rise in a warm, draft-free place for about 1 hour or until it doubles in volume.

Punch down the dough, place it on a lightly floured surface, and knead for 3 minutes. Divide the dough into 12 equal pieces. Shape each piece into a ball and place about 1 in apart, in three rows of four, onto the prepared baking sheet. Cover and leave to rise for about $1^1/_4$ hours until doubled in volume.

Combine the egg yolk with 1 tablespoon water in a bowl. Use a pastry brush to lightly brush the egg mixture on the top of each bun. Put the buns in the oven, reduce the temperature to 400°F, and bake for about 20 minutes until golden brown. Transfer to a wire rack.

In a small bowl combine the confectioners' sugar, remaining milk, and vanilla extract. Stir until smooth. When the buns have cooled slightly, drizzle a horizontal line across each row of buns followed by a vertical line to form a cross on the crown of each one.

OUR FAMED CARROT CAKE

This is most certainly the prized cake of our bakery.
Light, fluffy, and kissed with spices, you'll be licking
your lips and reaching for another slice!

Makes 1 cake

2/3 cup vegetable oil,
plus extra for greasing

3 eggs

1½ cups brown sugar

3 cups grated carrots

2/3 cup golden raisins

2/3 cup walnuts, chopped

1²/3 cups self-rising
flour

pinch of salt

½ teaspoon baking soda

1 teaspoon ground
cinnamon

1 teaspoon freshly
grated nutmeg

For the icing

1½ cups cream cheese,
chilled

5 tablespoons butter at
room temperature

1 teaspoon vanilla
extract

2½ cups confectioners'
sugar, sifted

finely grated zest of
1 orange

For decoration

walnuts

orange zest

Preheat the oven to 350°F. Oil a 5 × 9 in loaf pan and
line with parchment paper.

First make the cake. Beat the eggs in a large bowl,
then add the oil, brown sugar, grated carrot, raisins,
and chopped walnuts. Sift in the remaining ingredients
and bring the mixture together using a large spoon
until well combined.

Pour the mixture into the prepared loaf pan, smooth
the surface, and bake in the oven for 1¼ hours or
until a skewer inserted into the middle comes
out clean.

Remove from the oven and allow the cake to cool in the
pan for about 5 minutes before transferring it to a
wire rack to cool completely.

To make the icing, beat together the cream cheese and
butter in a bowl until well combined. Add the vanilla
extract, confectioners' sugar, and orange zest and mix
until the icing is smooth and thick. Use an offset
spatula to spread the icing evenly over the cooled
cake, dipping the spatula into a bowl of hot water if
the icing is hard to spread. Decorate the top of the
cake with walnuts and orange zest.

MINI CUPCAKES IN AN EGG BOX

How can any other Easter gift compare to these?
Too cute.

Makes 48 mini cupcakes

1½ sticks butter,
softened

⅔ cup superfine sugar

2 eggs

1 teaspoon vanilla
extract

⅔ cup milk

2 cups all-purpose flour,
sifted

1 teaspoon baking powder

For the icing

1½ sticks butter

1¼ cups confectioners'
sugar

1 teaspoon vanilla
extract

food coloring (optional)

To decorate and package. (optional)

lemon zest

chopped pistachios

chocolate flakes

seeds from vanilla pods

egg cartons

ribbon

Preheat the oven to 350°F. Line two 24-hole mini cupcake pans with paper baking cups and set aside.

In a bowl beat together the butter and sugar using an electric whisk. Add the eggs one at a time and continue to whisk until completely incorporated. Slowly pour in the milk, followed by the flour and baking powder, and whisk to combine.

Fill each paper cup with 1 tablespoon of the mixture and bake for about 10 minutes until a toothpick inserted into a cupcake center comes out clean. Allow to cool in the pans for 15 minutes, then transfer to a wire rack to cool completely before icing.

To make the icing beat together the butter, confectioners' sugar, and vanilla extract until thick and creamy. If you wish you can separate the icing out into different bowls and mix in different food colorings.

To ice the cupcakes, either pipe the icing onto the cakes using a piping bag or dip a spoon in hot water and smear the icing onto the cupcakes. Decorate with your choice of toppings.

Pop the mini cupcakes into the egg cartons, close, and tie with a pretty ribbon.

DANNY MEYER

Danny Meyer is a New York City restaurateur, author, and the CEO of Union Square Hospitality Group. He's a real New York icon and a huge inspiration to me. Any restaurant that Danny Meyers opens is a favorite of mine, from the fun Shake Shacks to the Union Square Café, but my favorite has always been Maialino, a fabulous Roman-style trattoria at the Gramercy Park Hotel. When I'm in New York I always try and eat at Maialino, and the last time I went for breakfast I enjoyed fantastic ricotta pancakes with poached eggs and tripe and great coffee.

My favorite time to go to Maialino is in the afternoon for a glass of wine and a few small bites from their bar menu, and I can't leave without having the Baccala, Cotiche Fritte (pork crackling), and their perfectly aged Pecorino cheese. Thank you to Danny and Executive Chef Nick Anderer for their delicious Bucatini All'Amatriciana recipe on page 103.

BUCATINI ALL'AMATRICIANA

Serves 2

½ cup guanciale or pancetta, diced

small red onion, diced

1 teaspoon dried red chile flakes

14-oz can whole peeled tomatoes

¾ cup bucatini or other long pasta

2 tablespoons olive oil

½ cup pecorino cheese, grated, plus extra to serve

salt and coarsely ground black pepper

Bring a large pan of salted water to a boil.

Meanwhile, gently sauté the guanciale or pancetta in a deep frying pan over medium heat until crisp and brown. Remove the guanciale or pancetta, leaving the fat behind, and set aside. Add the onions to the pan and sauté for several minutes over medium-low heat until soft.

Add salt (keeping in mind that the guanciale or pancetta will be salty), a generous amount of pepper, and the chile flakes, and gently cook for an additional 20 seconds, then add the tomatoes. Simmer for 10 minutes, breaking up the tomatoes with the back of a spoon as they cook, until the sauce thickens.

Meanwhile, drop the bucatini into the boiling water and cook until al dente. Drain, reserving a little of the cooking water, and add the pasta and reserved cooking water to the frying pan along with the guanciale or pancetta. Simmer gently, stirring continuously, for a minute or two or until the sauce begins to cling to the pasta.

Add the olive oil and the cheese, stirring well to combine. Serve with extra pecorino on the side.

LEMON ROASTED CHICKEN WITH OLIVE, BASIL, & TOMATO SAUCE AND PAN-FRIED GNOCCHI

I love the restaurant Baltazar in New York—the food and atmosphere are great. This my version of a delicious dish that I had the last time I was there.

Serves 4

4 garlic cloves, crushed
juice and zest of 1 lemon
4 tablespoons olive oil, plus extra for frying
2 chicken breasts, skin on, each breast cut in half
1¼ cups ripe plum tomatoes, halved
1 onion, finely chopped
20 black olives, halved
20 basil leaves
2 tablespoons butter
3¼ oz gnocchi
sea salt and freshly ground black pepper

Preheat the oven to 350°F.

Put 2 of the crushed garlic cloves into a large bowl with the lemon juice and zest, 2 tablespoons of the olive oil, and salt and pepper. Stir well to combine, then add the chicken and turn to coat. Cover the bowl and place in the fridge.

To make the tomato sauce, put the tomatoes, cut side up, into a roasting pan and sprinkle over the onion, remaining garlic, olives, basil, and the remaining olive oil. Season to taste and cook in the oven for 15 minutes or until the tomatoes have roasted.

Remove the chicken from the fridge and place, skin side down, in a hot frying pan for 3 minutes. Turn and cook for another 2 minutes. Transfer to a roasting pan and cook in the oven for 15 minutes.

Transfer the roasted tomatoes to a blender and blend to a smooth sauce.

Put a frying pan over medium heat and add the butter and a little olive oil. When the butter has melted, add in the gnocchi, season and cook, tossing every minute, for 5 minutes or until the gnocchi are golden brown.

Spoon a bed of the tomato sauce onto 4 plates, lay the chicken on top, and arrange the gnocchi around the chicken.

Makes 24 large cookies

2¾ cups all-purpose flour

1 teaspoon baking powder

1 teaspoon salt

2 sticks unsalted butter, room temperature

¾ cup peanut butter

2 teaspoons vanilla extract

1 cup brown sugar

½ cup superfine sugar

2 large eggs

PEANUT BUTTER

CHOCOLATE COOKIES

I never leave New York without a trip to Dean and Deluca on Broadway. You'll catch me gobbling their peanut butter cookies and stocking up on spices to bring home.

Preheat the oven to 350°F. Line two large baking sheets with parchment paper.

Mix together the flour, baking powder, and salt in a medium-sized bowl. Put the butter, peanut butter, and vanilla extract in a seperate bowl and beat using an electric whisk until well blended. Beat in both sugars, scraping down the sides of the bowl with a spatula.

Stir half of the dry ingredients into the peanut butter mixture. Add the eggs, one at a time, stirring well after each addition. Mix in the remaining dry ingredients.

Roll 2 heaping tablespoons of dough into a ball about 3 in across. Repeat to make around 24 cookies. Arrange the balls 3 in apart on the prepared baking sheets and use the back of a fork to flatten them. Bake in the oven for about 15 minutes until golden brown. Leave them to cool on the baking sheets for about 5 minutes, then use a spatula to transfer them to wire racks to cool completely.

Rose Sangria

MAY

MY BIRTHDAY

You know when your birthday is coming up and you secretly hope
something has been arranged? Well, a couple of years ago that didn't
happen to me. It was an incredibly busy time and my birthday just
came and went. I had cards and calls from family but there was no
actual celebration to mark the day. Boo hoo. I decided that would
never happen again. If I want to celebrate my birthday I will take
responsibility for it myself.

One year I had a tapas party. I whizz round so much with work I
don't always get a chance to catch up with friends, so tapas is a
perfect solution—delicious, easy to make, and an incredibly social
and relaxed way to eat. Because it was my birthday everyone was
happy to get involved, pushing the big table against the back wall,
decorating the room, and taking the dishes out afterward. I put a
big bowl of gazpacho in the center of the table and, to keep things
simple, I focused on just six tapas dishes but I made sure there
were plenty of them. One thing I learned
is that you can't have enough hot
chorizo, sliced thickly on toothpicks.
People love it.

This year, I had a girly lunch on my
actual birthday. It felt so sophisticated
and frothy. Cocktails with salads to
mitigate the sumptuous key lime pie for
dessert, and as a final little feminine
touch, banoffi pie cupcakes as favors for
my fabulous girlfriends. So if you don't
think your friends are organizing a
fabulous surprise party for your birthday
this year, why not do it yourself. Make
your birthday cake and eat it too!

Makes 1

lots of ice
2 tablespoons vodka
½ cup good-quality apple juice
thin slice of apple

APPLETINIS

A couple of years ago my friend Giana Ferguson (famed cheesemaker of Gubbeen cheese) made me a gin version of this drink, which also tasted delicious. Use good quality apple juice or make a sparkling version by using sparkling apple juice. It's a refreshing, perfect pre-lunch tipple!

Fill a cocktail shaker half full with ice and add the vodka and apple juice. Shake, pour, and garnish with a slice of apple.

CHICKEN CAESAR SALAD

Caesar salad is all about the dressing. My dressing is so simple to make and it will last in the fridge for about 10 days. I make versions of this salad with shrimp and pancetta at my restaurant Clodagh's Kitchen in Dublin. Just omit the chicken and replace with either pan-fried shrimp or crispy pancetta. I'm not a lover of croutons and prefer to serve a couple of grissini (breadsticks) with the salad.

Serves 2

1 tablespoon olive oil
2 chicken fillets
1 garlic clove, crushed
1 teaspoon chopped rosemary
10 very ripe cherry tomatoes, halved
20 Romaine lettuce leaves
1 heaping teaspoon pumpkin seeds
sea salt and freshly ground black pepper

For the dressing

2 tablespoons mayonnaise
1 tablespoon grated Parmesan cheese
1 garlic clove, crushed
1/4 teaspoon Dijon mustard
juice of 1/2 lemon

Preheat the oven to 400°F.

Put a frying pan over medium heat and add the oil. Leave to heat for 30 seconds, then add the chicken, season with salt and pepper, and sprinkle over the garlic and rosemary. Cook on each side for about 2 minutes until lightly golden. While the chicken is still cooking in the pan, carefully cut it into small pieces and continue to cook for another 3 minutes.

Meanwhile, make the Caesar dressing. Put all the ingredients in a blender and blend for 30 seconds.

When the chicken is cooked, remove it from the pan and keep warm in the oven. Add the cherry tomatoes to the frying pan and cook for 2 minutes.

Put the lettuce leaves in a large salad bowl, add the cooked chicken and tomatoes, pour over the dressing, and toss well. Sprinkle the pumpkin seeds on top.

CREAMY BASIL AND GRILLED CHICKEN TAGLIATELLE

This is wonderfully creamy but also sweet and fresh, thanks to the basil and tomatoes. Ideal for a girls' lunch or a speedy mid-week supper.

Serves 2

1 tablespoon olive oil
2 chicken cutlets
$2^{1}/_{3}$ cups rigatoni or penne pasta
12 cherry tomatoes
$^{2}/_{3}$ cup basil pesto
$^{3}/_{4}$ cup crème fraîche
$^{1}/_{2}$ cup Parmesan cheese, grated
sea salt and freshly ground black pepper

Put a frying pan over medium heat, add the oil, and leave to heat for 30 seconds. Add the chicken, season with salt and pepper, and cook on each side for 5 minutes or until lightly golden. Slice the seared chicken into small pieces and return to the pan.

Put a large saucepan of cold water over high heat, season with salt, cover, and bring to a boil. When the water is at a rolling boil, stir in the pasta and keep stirring for a minute so that the pasta shapes don't stick together.

Cut the tomatoes in half, add them to the frying pan with the chicken, and cook for another 5 minutes.

Mix together the pesto and crème fraîche and stir into the pan with the chicken and tomatoes. Reduce the heat and simmer for 5 minutes.

Drain the pasta and return it to the saucepan. Add the chicken and sauce, stir well, and season to taste with salt and pepper. Serve in two large, warm pasta bowls with the grated Parmesan.

BANOFFEE PIE CUPCAKES

Wickedly good, I remember the morning when we perfected this recipe in my bakery and that sublime first bite.

Makes 12

For the cupcakes
2 eggs

6 tablespoons butter

²/₃ cup superfine sugar

1 teaspoon ground cinnamon

3 very ripe bananas, mashed

1¼ cups self-rising flour, sifted

1 teaspoon baking powder

For the caramel
1 cup sugar

6 tablespoons butter

½ cup heavy cream

For the icing
6 tablespoons butter

⅓ cup superfine sugar

Preheat the oven to 350°F. Line a 12-hole cupcake pan with paper baking cups.

To make the caramel, put the sugar, butter, and cream in a saucepan over medium heat, stirring all the time. When the mixture has come to a boil, reduce the heat and stop stirring.

To make the cupcakes, whisk together the eggs, butter, and sugar until light and fluffy. Add the cinnamon and bananas, then fold in the flour, baking powder, and three-quarters of the caramel.

Spoon the mixture into paper baking cups until they are about two-thirds full and bake in the oven for 15 minutes. Transfer to a wire rack to cool.

Meanwhile, make the icing. Whisk together the butter and sugar with the remaining caramel. Pipe the icing onto the cooled cakes.

KEY LIME PIE

This should take you no longer than 15 minutes to prepare. You can accessorize the base with hazelnuts or pine nuts, but the filling is perfect and has no need to be dressed in any way. Make the pie the day before you wish to eat it and it will taste even better. It will keep for five days in the fridge.

Serves 8-10

Preheat the oven to 350°F. Grease a 9-in springform cake pan.

For the base

12 graham crackers
$1/4$ cup superfine sugar
$1^{1}/_{4}$ sticks butter, melted, plus extra for greasing

First make the base. Put the graham crackers, superfine sugar, and melted butter in a food processor and blend together for 2 minutes. Transfer the pie base to the pan and press down with the back of a spoon.

For the filling

4 egg yolks
$1^{2}/_{3}$ cups condensed milk
juice and zest of 5 limes

To make the filling, whisk the egg yolks in a bowl, then gradually whisk in the condensed milk until smooth. Mix in the lime juice. Pour the filling onto the graham cracker base and cook in the oven for 15-20 minutes. Transfer to a wire rack to cool.

Sprinkle the lime zest over the pie and serve chilled.

CHOCOLATE BIRTHDAY CAKE

This is so so simple to make. The cake is lovely and light whereas the icing is rich and fudgy. It will last for 4 days in the fridge, but hopefully it won't last one day!

Makes 1 cake

For the cake

$2\frac{1}{2}$ cups all-purpose flour, plus extra for flouring

1 teaspoon baking powder

1 teaspoon baking soda

$\frac{3}{4}$ cup cocoa powder

$1\frac{1}{4}$ cups sugar

$1\frac{1}{2}$ sticks butter, plus extra for greasing

4 eggs

$1\frac{1}{2}$ cups milk

2 teaspoons vanilla extract

For the icing

1 cup cream cheese, softened

4 tablespoons butter, softened

3 tablespoons milk

$2\frac{1}{4}$ cups superfine sugar

1 cup cocoa powder

2 teaspoons vanilla extract

Lightly grease and flour two 8-in round cake pans.

First make the cake. Sift the flour into the bowl of a mixer, then add the remaining ingredients. Mix, first on low speed then increasing to medium, for 4 minutes until the ingredients are well combined.

Divide the mixture between the 2 pans and tap gently to remove any air bubbles. Cook in the oven for 45 minutes or until a toothpick inserted into the center comes out clean. Allow the cakes to cool in the pans for 15 minutes before removing to a wire rack and leaving to cool completely.

While the cake is cooling, make the icing. Whisk all the ingredients together to form a delicious light, fudgy icing.

Ice the bottom half of the cake and sandwich the two cakes together, then completely smother with icing.

ROSE SANGRIA

This drink goes down so well, just remember to share it! Try using sparkling wine for a more fun sangria. It needs to be served very cold so add lots of ice to the mix before serving in chilled glasses. I always pop my glasses in the freezer for 30 minutes before use.

Serves 8

1 bottle chilled rosé wine
1 cup Cointreau
2 limes, thinly sliced
2 oranges, thinly sliced
16 raspberries, quartered
1 quart sparkling water
lots of ice

Stir together the wine, Cointreau, limes, oranges, raspberries, and sparkling water. Add the ice and serve in iced glasses.

SPANISH SPICY GARLIC SHRIMP

For a more sophisticated dish, serve the shrimp on slices of toasted baguette brushed with olive oil, or for more of a kick try chile oil.

Serves 10

8 tablespoons extra virgin olive oil

8 garlic cloves, chopped

3 chiles (hot or mild, to taste), seeded and chopped

2 tablespoons smoked paprika (or standard paprika)

1 onion, finely chopped

2¼ lb raw peeled large shrimp

Heat the oil over gentle heat and add the garlic, chiles, paprika, and onion. Cook until the onion is soft, without any color.

Add the shrimp to the pan and increase the heat slightly. Cook for 5-10 minutes or until the shrimp have turned dark pink.

Serve with crusty bread to mop up the flavorsome juices.

CROQUETTES

These are a real crowd-pleaser and taste even better if you prepare them the night before and let them set in the fridge overnight before cooking.

Serves 8

1½ cups mashed potato
1 teaspoon Dijon mustard
1 teaspoon finely chopped flat-leaf parsley
7 oz cooked ham, cut into small pieces
1 cup Gruyère cheese, grated
1 egg, beaten
2 cups fine breadcrumbs
olive oil
sea salt and freshly ground black pepper

Preheat the oven to 400°F.

Put the mashed potato, mustard, chopped parsley, cooked ham, and cheese in a large bowl and mix well.

Use a tablespoon to scoop the mixture into cork-like shapes. Lay them on a tray and use a pastry brush to coat each all over with beaten egg. Scatter the breadcrumbs on a large plate and, one by one, gently roll the croquettes in the crumbs.

Fry the croquettes in a frying pan in hot oil, turning them once, until they are golden; alternatively, bake them in the oven for 15 minutes.

TAPENADE TOASTS

Try adding a sliver of Manchego cheese, a teaspoon of soft goat cheese, or cured ham on top of the toasts.

Serves 10

14 oz pitted black olives

9 oz capers, pressed in paper towels to remove excess vinegar

2 oz anchovy fillets, drained

4 garlic cloves

3 tablespoons extra virgin olive oil, plus extra for brushing

juice of 1 lemon

1 baguette, sliced

Put the olives, capers, anchovies, garlic, oil, and lemon juice in a food processor and blend to a thickish paste, adding more oil if required.

Toast the bread and brush with olive oil. Smear the tapenade on top of the toast and serve.

GAZPACHO

I love serving gazpacho in chilled shot glasses. You can make this ahead and store in a fridge. If your gazpacho gets too thick just whisk in more chilled water.

Serves 8

2¼ cups ripe tomatoes, skinned and chopped

2 garlic cloves, crushed

1 red bell pepper, chopped

1 onion, chopped

1 slice of good-quality stale white bread, sliced

1 cup cold water

2 tablespoons olive oil

2 tablespoons white wine vinegar

sea salt and freshly ground black pepper

For the garnish

½ cucumber, diced

2 scallions, finely chopped

Put all the ingredients into a food processor and process until completely smooth. Transfer to a bowl, cover, and leave to chill in the fridge.

Serve chilled, garnished with cucumber and scallions.

TRADITIONAL SPANISH TORTILLA

Try adding chorizo, pancetta, tomatoes, or prosciutto to this fab recipe. It's delicious served cold with a drizzle of homemade mayonnaise or tomato salsa, too.

Serves 2

2 tablespoons olive oil
1 onion, halved and thinly sliced
²/₃ lb potatoes, peeled and diced
6 eggs, beaten
sea salt and freshly ground black pepper

Place a large frying pan over medium heat and add 1 tablespoon of the oil. When the oil is hot add the onion and potatoes, reduce the heat, and allow to cook for 15 minutes, stirring the pan every few minutes.

When the onion and potatoes are cooked, put them into a bowl with the eggs. Season with salt and pepper and mix together.

Place the frying pan over low heat and add the remaining oil. Pour in the egg mixture and leave to cook for about 15 minutes or until the egg is set.

To flip the tortilla over, put a plate over the pan and turn the pan over so that the tortilla comes out on the plate. Slide the tortilla back into the pan, cooked side up, and return to the heat for another 5 minutes.

You can eat the tortilla hot or cold. It's delicious with a green salad.

SEAFOOD PAELLA

The first time I tasted Paella was in the La Brecha food market in San Sebastian. It really is the best party food and can be made with many different types of fish.

Serves 10

olive oil, for frying
8-in piece of chorizo, diced
(I love Gubbeen chorizo from Ireland)
2 onions, diced
4 garlic cloves, crushed
2½ cups paella rice
2 teaspoons paprika
1 quart hot fish stock
pinch of saffron
1 lb monkfish, chopped
2¼ lb mussels, cleaned and debearded
10 unshelled raw shrimp
6 red piquillo peppers
sea salt and freshly ground black pepper
2 lemons, cut into wedges, to serve

Heat a large paella pan over medium heat. Add a little olive oil and the chorizo. Leave to cook for about 5 minutes until the chorizo begins to crisp, then add the onions and garlic. Cook for another 10 minutes.

Stir in the rice and season with salt and pepper. Add the paprika, stock, and saffron and leave to simmer for about 15 minutes.

Scatter the pieces of monkfish over the rice and push them under the surface with the back of a spoon. Lay the mussels and shrimp over the top and simmer for another 5 minutes. Lay the piquillo peppers on top to warm through. Cook for another 5 minutes or until the mussels have opened and the shrimp are pink. Discard any mussels that remain closed. Serve with lemon wedges around the pan.

TIPS

You can add mussels, clams, hake—practically any kind of fish—to this dish. If you can't get your hands on piquillo peppers, core, seed, and slice some ordinary red bell peppers and add them along with the onions.

MOROCCAN ORANGE CAKE

This, I guarantee, will be one of your favorite recipes in this book. Light, moist, and so zingy, it will keep for up to a week in an airtight container.

Serves 8

1/2 cup slightly stale white breadcrumbs

1 cup superfine sugar

1 cup ground almonds

1 teaspoon baking powder

3/4 cup sunflower oil

4 eggs

finely grated zest of 1 large unwaxed orange

finely grated zest of 1 unwaxed lemon

whipped cream or Greek yogurt, to serve (optional)

For the citrus syrup

juice of 1 orange

juice of 1 lemon

1/3 cup superfine sugar

1 cinnamon stick

2 cloves

Preheat the oven to 350°F. Line the base, grease, and flour an 8 × 2-in round cake pan.

Mix together the breadcrumbs, sugar, almonds, and baking powder. Whisk the oil with the eggs, then pour the egg mixture into the dry ingredients and mix well. Add the orange and lemon zests. Pour the mixture into the cake pan and cook in the oven for 45-60 minutes or until the cake is golden brown. Check that the cake is cooked by inserting a skewer into the center; if it's ready the skewer should come out clean. Allow to cool for 5 minutes before turning out onto a wire rack.

Meanwhile, make the citrus syrup. Put all the ingredients into a saucepan and bring gently to a boil, stirring until the sugar has dissolved completely. Simmer for 3 minutes. Remove the cinnamon stick and cloves from the syrup.

While the cake is still warm, pierce it several times with a skewer, then spoon the hot syrup over the cake, allowing it to run into the holes. Leave to cool. Spoon any excess syrup back over the cake every now and then until it is all soaked up. Serve with whipped cream or a dollop of thick Greek yogurt, if you like.

Potted Shrimp

Sparking Summer Berry Gelatins

JUNE

SUMMER PICNICS

June is the start of the big summer sporting events. I love tennis but my real passion is the races— Punchestown, Leopardstown, Galway, and, of course, Royal Ascot. The horses are so beautiful, the actual races are ridiculously exciting, but for me the best thing is the picnic. I love seeing people in the parking lot, the trunk open, serving the most sumptuous feasts off the top of the spare tire. In this chapter I wanted to look at picnic food that isn't just a few snacks but a proper lunch, worthy of the sport of kings.

The trick is to choose food that travels well. To avoid things getting soggy, keep your chutneys, relishes, and pickles away from the bread and dressing away from the salad until you are ready to eat. Same with cucumber and tomato, chop them just before serving to avoid watery salads. Keep dishes with a strong or pungent smell wrapped and sealed and make sure your ice packs are frozen hard to keep everything fresh.

A really elegant way to start the picnic is with potted shrimp. Little brown shrimps boiled in spiced sea water on board the boats, then sealed in butter. Serve with Melba toast and a squeeze of fresh lemon. Cold meats, whole cooked salmon, and quiches travel well and are delicious with salads. A great cheese course always works but not at the expense of something sweet and yummy, and if you serve the sweet stuff with tea, it has to come from a pot and use loose leaf tea, not bags. Just don't get so into the picnic you forget to make a bet!

Makes about 1 lb
3²/₃ cups pasta flour
a large pinch of salt
2 medium eggs
semolina flour, for
dusting

FRESH PASTA

The feeling of achievement when you roll
a pasta sheet into tagliatelle is
fantastic. It takes a few goes to get
the hang of it but once you have,
there's no stopping how creative you
can be. Happy pasta making!

Put the flour, salt, and eggs in a food processor and
blend together until a dough forms. Put the dough on a
floured board and knead until smooth. Separate the dough
into six balls, cover with a kitchen towel, and allow to
rest in a cool place or in the fridge for 30 minutes.

If you have a pasta machine, set it up and push the
dough through the roller. With each pass through the
rollers reduce the setting, until you reach the final
setting. Be careful that your pasta does not break as
you should now have a long, thin sheet.

If you don't have a pasta maker you need to roll the
dough out very thinly with a rolling pin. (This can be
hard as it breaks easily, and if you intend to make a
lot of pasta I would recommend buying a pasta maker
because they are inexpensive and so useful.) Dust
lightly with semolina flour and hang over a clean clothes
rack or something similar for 10 minutes.

Store in the fridge and eat within 2 days.
To make **lasagna sheets**, cut the pasta into suitably sized
rectangles.
To make **tagliatelle**, cut into ¹/₂-in strips.
For **tagliolini**, cut the dough into ¹/₄-in strips.
For **pappardelle**, cut the dough into ³/₄-in strips

FLAVORED FRESH PASTA

For **spinach pasta**, take 5 cups of spinach and blanch in boiling water for 1 minute, drain, and squeeze dry. Add to the flour and egg and proceed as on page 134.

For **tomato pasta**, add 2 tablespoons of tomato paste to the flour and egg and proceed as on page 134.

For **herb pasta**, add 4 tablespoons of finely chopped herbs of your choice (such as basil, fresh cilantro, or oregano) to the flour and egg and proceed as on page 134.

For **black ink pasta**, add 3 tablespoons of squid ink to the flour and egg and blend as on page 134; you may need to add a little more flour if the dough is too moist.

To cook the pasta: The best way to cook your pasta is to get the largest saucepan that you have and fill it with cold water and a good pinch of salt. Cover and bring to a boil. Once the water is at a rolling boil put the pasta into the water and stir immediately for 2 minutes so that the pasta pieces do not stick together. Cooking times vary depending on the shape and size of the pasta, so the best way to check it is to taste it. The pasta should be slightly al dente because it will continue to cook after it has been drained. Drain the pasta, reserving about 2 tablespoons of the cooking water, and return the drained pasta to the saucepan (off the heat). Stir in the 2 tablespoons of cooking water, followed by your pasta sauce.

THREE CHEESE RAVIOLI

You can play around with the combinations of ricotta and spinach, smoked salmon, and soft goat cheese. The ravioli freezes well, so you can make ahead. I love to serve this with a fresh sun-dried tomato pesto or my creamy walnut and cilantro pesto (see page 211).

Serves 2

½ cup ricotta

½ cup Parmesan cheese, grated

½ cup Fontina cheese, grated

½ teaspoon dried oregano

1 tablespoon finely torn basil

1 batch of homemade fresh pasta (see page 134)

sea salt and freshly ground black pepper

In a medium bowl mix together the ricotta, Fontina, Parmesan, oregano, and basil and season with salt and pepper.

Use a 3in cookie cutter to cut out circles from your pasta sheets. Put about 2 teaspoons of filling in the center of half the pasta circles, leaving a clear edge around the perimeter. Dip a pastry brush in water and lightly brush around the edges of each circle. Put one of the remaining pasta shapes on top and press the edges together to seal around the filling, being careful to press out any excess air.

Bring a large saucepan of salted water to a boil. Cook the ravioli for about 5 minutes or until al dente. Serve with Creamy Walnut and Cilantro Pesto (see page 211) or Olive, Basil, and Tomato Sauce (see pages 104).

CREAMY TOMATO AND SPINACH PASTA

A lovely, light summer dish—perfect for enjoying al fresco with a chilled white wine.

Serves 6

olive oil, for frying
1 onion, thinly sliced
2 cloves garlic, peeled and finely sliced
2 x 14-oz cans good-quality plum tomatoes, chopped
8 basil leaves
5³/₄ cups penne pasta
2 pats of butter
8 large handfuls of spinach, washed and drained
¹/₄ of a nutmeg, grated
2²/₃ cups crumbly ricotta cheese
sea salt and freshly ground black pepper
2 handfuls of freshly grated Parmesan cheese to serve

Bring a large saucepan of salted water to a boil.

Meanwhile, make the tomato sauce. Heat about a tablespoon of olive oil in a saucepan over low heat and add the onion and garlic. Leave to cook for a minute then stir in the tomatoes and basil and season with salt and pepper. Reduce the heat and allow to simmer for 10 minutes or until thickened.

Stir the pasta into the boiling water and leave to cook according to the package instructions until al dente. Drain and set aside.

Heat the butter in a frying pan over medium heat and add a handful of spinach and the nutmeg. Cook the spinach, turning continuously, until wilted, then add the remaining spinach, a handful at a time, and cook until wilted.

Finely chop the cooked spinach and add it to the pan with the tomato sauce. Crumble over the ricotta and stir in the pasta. Mix well to combine and serve with the Parmesan.

CRAB CAKES WITH LIME AND TOMATO GUACAMOLE

If you have the time, once you have shaped your crab cakes allow them 30 minutes in the fridge to set. They freeze extremely well. A perfect summer lunch dish, served with a big green salad.

Makes 4 cakes

2 slices of good-quality bread, made into rough breadcrumbs

³/₄ lb white crab meat

2 tablespoons mayonnaise

drop of Worcestershire sauce

1 tablespoon olive oil

1 teaspoon finely chopped dill

juice and zest of 1 lemon

butter, for frying

sea salt and freshly ground black pepper

Put all the ingredients, except the butter, in a bowl and season to taste with salt and pepper. Mix well and form the crab mixture into 4 round patties.

Put a frying or griddle pan over medium heat and add the butter. When the butter begins to foam add the crab cakes and cook for 3 minutes. Turn them over and cook for another 2 minutes. They should be golden in color.

Serve with Lime Guacamole.

For the Lime Guacamole

1 ripe avocado

1 ripe plum tomato

1 garlic clove, crushed

2 tablespoons freshly squeezed lime juice

1 tablespoon extra virgin olive oil

1 tablespoon chopped fresh cilantro

sea salt and freshly ground black pepper

Cut the avocado in half and discard the pit. Scoop out the flesh and cut it into small cubes. Chop the plum tomatoes into similar sized cubes.

Put the tomato and avocado in a bowl, mix in the garlic, lime juice, olive oil, and cilantro and mix together well. Season to taste with salt and pepper. Cover with plastic wrap immediately because the avocado will quickly discolor.

TIP

To keep your
guacamole nice
and green, place
the avocado pit
on top of the dip
and cover with
plastic wrap
before chilling.

SCOTCH EGGS

This year was the first time that I made Scotch eggs, and I am now a lifetime member of the Scotch egg fan club! They do take a bit of time to make but they are so worth it.

Makes 4

4 eggs
8 oz sausage meat
1 teaspoon finely chopped thyme leaves
1 tablespoon finely chopped flat-leaf parsley
1 teaspoon Dijon mustard
zest of 1 lemon
1 scallion, finely chopped
1 egg, beaten
1 cup all-purpose flour
1 cup very fine breadcrumbs
canola or sunflower oil, for shallow frying
sea salt and freshly ground black pepper

Put the eggs in a pan of cold water over high heat and bring to a boil. Reduce the heat and simmer for exactly 7 minutes. Drain and cool the eggs under cold running water, then remove the shells.

Put the sausage meat in a large mixing bowl with the thyme, parsley, mustard, lemon zest, and scallion. Season with salt and pepper and mix well together until the ingredients are combined.

Dust your hands with flour and take a quarter of the sausage mixture at a time. Roll the meat into a ball and put it on a piece of plastic wrap and press slightly. Cover with another sheet of plastic wrap and gently roll out into a circle about 2 in across.

Remove the top sheet of plastic wrap and put a boiled egg in the center of the sausage mixture circle. Close the sausage mixture around the egg using the plastic wrap underneath as an aid and reshape until you have the perfect egg shape. Remove all the plastic wrap. Repeat with the remaining eggs and sausage mixture.

Put the beaten egg in one bowl and the breadcrumbs in another bowl. Dip each Scotch egg into the beaten egg, then roll it in the breadcrumbs.

Put a shallow pan over medium heat and pour in the oil until it is about two-thirds full. When it is hot carefully drop in the Scotch eggs and fry them for 10 minutes, turning every few minutes to make sure they are evenly fried. Remove from the oil and drain on paper towels. Serve at room temperature.

Serves 2

4½ sticks butter
1 teaspoon cayenne pepper
1 lb brown shrimp or small
shrimp

POTTED SHRIMP

There is something wonderfully decadent about opening
a Mason jar of potted shrimp at a picnic and scooping
it onto crispy Melba toast or crackers. They will last
for up to 2 weeks in the fridge.

Clarify the butter by gently melting it in a saucepan. Once the butter
has melted leave it to sit for about 4 minutes to separate. Skim off
the foam that rises to the top and gently pour or spoon the clear
butter off the top, leaving behind the milk solids, which will be at
the bottom of the pan. The clear butter is the clarified butter. Mix
the cayenne pepper with the clarified butter.

Cook the shrimps by placing them in a saucepan of boiling water
and simmering for 5 minutes. The shrimps will turn pink when they
are cooked. Drain and shell the shrimps, by twisting the head to
remove it and pulling off the legs. Hold the tail and pull off the
remaining shell.

Put the shelled shrimps in a sterilized jar and pour the clarified
butter on top, making sure that the shrimps are completely covered.
Leave to set in the fridge for 1 hour.

SMOKED SALMON PATE

This takes minutes to make, but you do need a good quality smoked salmon. Spread on brown soda bread, toast, or crackers.

Serves 6

9 oz smoked salmon
½ cup cream cheese
¼ cup crème fraîche
juice and zest of
1 lemon
1 teaspoon capers
freshly ground black
pepper

Put all the ingredients except the pepper into a food processor and blend until smooth. Season with pepper to taste.

Transfer to a bowl and chill.

PIMM'S

I love to go to the races and a trip to the racecourse wouldn't be right without a glass of chilled Pimm's!

Serves 6

³/₄ cup Pimm's No. 1
2¹/₂ cups lemonade
¹/₂ cucumber, sliced
6 strawberries, hulled and halved
1 lemon, cut into wedges
1 orange, cut into wedges
ice

Put all the ingredients in a punch bowl or large jug and mix well.

LEMON SHORTBREAD

You can make lots of variations of this recipe. Try replacing the lemon zest with orange zest or finely chopped pine nuts.

Makes 10–12

2 sticks butter, softened
¹/₂ cup superfine sugar
zest of 1 lemon
¹/₂ teaspoon vanilla extract
3 cups all-purpose flour, sifted, plus extra for dusting

Preheat the oven to 325°F. Line a baking sheet with parchment paper.

Cream the butter and sugar together in a large bowl. Add the lemon zest and vanilla extract and blend well. Stir in the flour a little at a time. The dough will be crumbly, so pour it out onto a lightly floured surface and work it together by hand until smooth. Pat or roll out the dough to a rectangle about ¹/₂-in thick. Cut into small squares, rectangles, or diamonds, whichever you prefer.

Arrange the cookies on the baking sheet and bake in the oven for 20-25 minutes until the edges are just starting to brown.

SPARKING SUMMER BERRY GELATINS

Prosecco adds a lovely sparkle to this summer berry gelatin, but for a nonalcoholic version you can just use water instead.

Makes 6

1½ cups boiling water
¼ cup superfine sugar
6 mint or sweet geranium leaves
2 cups prosecco (or sparkling wine)
4 teaspoons of gelatin
1⅓ cups mixed summer berries (such as raspberries, blueberries, and quartered strawberries)

First make a sugar syrup. Put the hot water and sugar in a small saucepan over low to medium heat, stirring until all the sugar is dissolved, then increase the heat and bring to a boil. Turn down the heat, add the mint or sweet geranium leaves, and simmer for 4 minutes.

Pour the wine into a large bowl and add the gelatin. Leave for about 5 minutes or until the gelatin is dissolved. Add the gelatin to the sugar syrup. Whisk the syrup until the gelatin has completely dissolved, then pour the syrup back into the bowl with the sparkling wine and whisk to combine. Remove the mint leaves, leave to cool completely, then refrigerate the gelatin for about 1 hour.

As soon as the gelatin starts to thicken, stir in the summer berries. Divide the gelatin between 6 glasses and refrigerate for 4 hours or until they have completely set.

KIDS' LEMONADE ICE POPS

4 lemons
2 oranges
1½ quarts water

For the stock syrup

1½ cups sugar
½ quart water
5 sweet geranium leaves

First make the stock syrup. Dissolve the sugar in the water over gentle heat. Add the geranium leaves and bring to a boil. Boil for 2 minutes then allow to cool.

Juice the fruit and mix well with the stock syrup, adding water to taste. Pour the mixture into popsicle containers and freeze for 1 hour.

WHITE CHOCOLATE AND PASSION FRUIT CHEESECAKE

Sumptuous and creamy, this is one of my favorite desserts to eat in the summer. The hazelnuts in the base add a lovely crunch to the cake. It will last for about five days stored in the fridge.

Makes 1 cake (serves 10)

3 cups graham crackers, broken up into pieces

1/2 cup hazelnuts

1 1/2 sticks of butter, melted

1 cup ricotta

1 cup cream cheese, softened

6 1/3 oz white chocolate, chopped

1/2 cup superfine sugar

zest of 1 lemon

3 eggs

3/4 cup passion fruit pulp (from about 12 passion fruit)

Preheat the oven to 350°F. Lightly grease a 9-in springform cake or tart pan.

Put the graham crackers and hazelnuts in a food processor and process until they resemble fine breadcrumbs. Add the butter and mix to combine. Press the mixture into the cake or tart pan and refrigerate for 30 minutes or until firm and cold.

Put the ricotta, cream cheese, white chocolate, superfine sugar, and lemon zest in the bowl of a food processor and process until smooth. Gradually add the eggs, processing well after each addition. Fold through the passion fruit pulp and pour the mixture over the base. Bake for 30-35 minutes or until set and allow to cool completely before serving.

MINI VICTORIA SPONGES

These are the cutest little cakes in the world! They are so simple to make yet look and taste divine.

Makes 6

5 tablespoons unsalted butter, softened, plus extra for greasing
¾ cup superfine sugar
3 medium eggs
1 teaspoon vanilla extract
1½ cups self-rising flour, sifted
1 teaspoon baking powder, sifted
confectioners' sugar, for dusting

For the filling

1¼ cups whipping cream
½ cup confectioners' sugar plus extra for dusting
12-oz jar strawberry jam

Preheat the oven to 350°F. Butter and lightly dust six individual pans, each about 3 in across and 2 in high, with flour.

Put the butter in a large mixing bowl with the sugar and beat together with an electric whisk until light and fluffy.

Slowly beat in the eggs, one at a time, followed by the vanilla extract. When the eggs are fully incorporated, fold in the flour and baking powder.

Spoon the cake mixture evenly into the baking pans and tap the sides to release any air bubbles. Bake in the oven for 20 minutes or until the cakes are lightly golden brown. Check by inserting a skewer into the middle of the cake; if it comes out clean the cake is cooked. Remove from the oven and allow to cool in the pans for about 15 minutes before removing them from the pans and transferring them to a wire rack to cool completely.

Meanwhile, lightly whip the cream and confectioners' sugar together until light and fluffy. Cut the cooled cakes in half horizontally through the center, then spread a generous amount of strawberry jam on the top of the bottom halves, followed by the whipped cream. Put the top halves of the cakes on top and lightly dust with confectioners' sugar.

gourmet mini burgers

JULY

BARBECUE TIME!

I have a photo of my 10 year old self in flowery wellies, standing next to a barbecue, rain dripping off my hood. In my hand is a white bun, a blackened sausage poking out of the end. I am wearing a huge grin, smeared in tomato sauce. We often had to bolt from the rain and the sausages, burgers, and chicken drumsticks were always incinerated (to avoid food poisoning). But to my 10-year-old palate they were totally delicious.

A foreign exchange visit to stay with the Famille Ronsin in Chateaubourg in France changed everything. Madame Ronsin was a fabulous cook who loved to barbecue. She served barbecued meat, medium rare. It was delicious and no one died from eating it. At the seaside we had barbecued squid with chile and crunchy sea salt, gigantic shrimp with olive oil and parsley. But the thing I couldn't wait to tell my mum—she barbecued vegetables! Tomatoes, asparagus, mushrooms the size of umbrellas; even green beans were lightly charred and tossed in olive oil. And fruit: peaches, threaded with a rosemary stem, splashed with Marsala, charred and served with a dollop of mascarpone.

The secret to M. Ronsin's elegant, relaxed barbecues was to prepare ahead and keep it simple. Marinate the meat and fish the night before, get the kids to make three fresh salads, *et voila*, ready to roll.

What I learned from my childhood barbecues in Cork and from M. Ronsin, is that barbecue is an attitude. Be creative, try something new, but don't get too complicated. Focus on what really matters, fun; enjoying good food with great friends in a relaxed, informal atmosphere.

MEAT

In my early twenties I worked at the White Dog, Nantucket Island, in the US for a summer while I was in college. I was working flat out with a mainly Irish staff. At elevenish we'd knock off, grab some burgers and steaks from the kitchen, and head for the beach. By the light of car headlights we'd fire up a grill, plonk an old boombox on a rock and dance like madmen. When the coals were hot we'd grill the steaks and burgers and eat like it was our last meal on earth.

The great thing with grilling is, being outside, you can get really smoky. The smoke not only adds great flavor to the meat but also helps cook it. Remember to sear the meat over the hottest part of the grill then move the coals to the side so that it can slow cook over a lower heat. This allows the meat to retain more moisture.

I've included a couple of recipes for rubs and marinades in this chapter but I really encourage you to experiment and create your own. Most of us have all the spices we need for a good rub, hiding away in our kitchen cabinets. Make sure you rub the spices in thoroughly and give the meat time to absorb the flavor. If I'm using a marinade I like to leave it overnight in the fridge.

All the barbecue gadgetry and gourmet recipes can make it seem a little stressful. In fact grilling is essentially the simplest form of cooking; perfect for nervous or novice cooks. So get out there and have a go.

FISH

The best grilled squid I ever had was in Greece.
My friend and I took the ferry to the island of
Alonissos, following the local fishing boats into
harbor. After touring around on a couple of
battered old Vespas, looking for a room to rent,
I was starving. Right on cue the wonderful singed,
briny smell of grilled squid wafted in the bedroom
window. We followed our noses down onto the street
and bought a plateful from the vendor. It was
served with just a squeeze of lemon and a sprinkle
of salt and it tasted like heaven. My mouth is
watering just remembering it. It was the freshness
of the squid that was so good, straight off the
fishing boats we docked with. That is the key to a
great fish barbecue—freshness.

When I lived in West Cork I used to go fishing,
usually the catch was mackerel or pollock, both
sustainable. I'd take my fish straight to shore,
fillet it, and cook it on a little disposable grill,
you can get them for next to nothing. I have never
had fish in a restaurant that tasted as good as the
fish I ate on that West Cork beach! The less time the
fish spends between leaving the sea and reaching your
plate the more sensational the taste.

If you can't go fishing yourself (and I do recommend
it), find a good fishmonger. Don't be afraid to ask
what's fresh in that day. The fish eyes should be
bright, the skin should shine and most importantly
it should smell like fresh sea water.

ASIAN MARINADE

Makes approximately 1 cup

$1/2$ cup sunflower oil
$1/4$ cup rice wine vinegar
3 tablespoons soy sauce
3 tablespoons chopped fresh ginger
2 tablespoons sugar

Whisk the ingredients together in a bowl. Great with white fish.

INDIAN MARINADE

Makes approximately $3/4$ cup

$1/2$ cup yogurt
2 tablespoons sunflower oil
1 teaspoon ground cumin
1 teaspoon ground turmeric
$1/2$ teaspoon ground coriander
1 tablespoon chopped fresh coriander

Whisk the ingredients together in a bowl. This is perfect for lamb and chicken.

SPICY MARINADE

Makes approximately $3/4$ cup

$1/2$ cup olive oil
2 tablespoons lemon juice
2 tablespoons Dijon mustard
$1/2$ teaspoon crushed red pepper flakes

Whisk the ingredients together in a bowl. Works well with beef and pork.

juice and zest of 1 lime
1 small red chile, finely chopped
$1/4$ cup extra virgin olive oil
16 medium-sized shrimp, shelled and
deveined
1 teaspoon of Dijon mustard
7 oz arugula leaves
1 avocado, peeled and diced
1 large ripe mango, peeled and diced
sea salt and freshly ground black pepper

SUMMER GRILLED SHRIMP,
AVOCADO, AND MANGO SALAD

Grab a bag of fresh shrimp, put together the marinade, get
the salad ready, and fire up the barbecue grill!

To make the marinade, mix together half the lime juice and
zest, the chile, and half the olive oil. Season with salt and
pepper and add the shrimp, tossing them to coat completely.
Leave to marinate for 15 minutes.

If you are using bamboo skewers, now is the time to soak them
in water for 15 minutes so that they do not burn while the
food cooks. Thread the marinated shrimp onto the skewers.

Heat the broiler or grill to medium, or put a frying pan or
griddle pan over medium heat. Grill, broil, or fry the shrimp
for about 1 minute each side until they are pink and cooked
through. Set aside and keep warm.

To make the salad dressing, whisk the Dijon mustard with the
remaining lime juice and zest and olive oil. Season with salt
and pepper. Arrange the arugula, avocado, and mango on a
serving plate, place the shrimp skewers on top, drizzle with
the dressing, and serve.

ITALIAN ORZO PASTA SALAD

If you can't get your hands on orzo pasta, which is
a tiny pasta shaped like rice, you can substitute it
with penne pasta. It will last for approximately
3 days in the fridge.

Serves 4

2⅓ cups orzo

2 tablespoons balsamic vinegar

4 tablespoons extra virgin olive oil

1 garlic clove, crushed

¼ red onion, finely diced

12 sun-dried tomatoes, finely chopped

4 Kalamata olives, pitted and sliced

a small bunch fresh basil, leaves torn

2 tablespoons pine nuts, toasted

sea salt and freshly ground black pepper

First cook the orzo. Fill a large saucepan with salted water, bring to a boil, add the orzo, and cook for 8-10 minutes until tender. Drain.

While still hot, toss the orzo in a bowl with the balsamic vinegar, olive oil, and garlic. Season to taste with salt and pepper.

Allow the orzo to cool and then mix in a large serving bowl with the onion, sun-dried tomatoes, olives, basil, and pine nuts. Serve immediately.

GREEK SALAD

I often substitute the feta for my local feta-style cheese, which is called Knocklara. It's so creamy and crumbly, much better than the highly processed feta that you find in some supermarkets.

Serves 4

4 tablespoons extra virgin olive oil

2 tablespoons lemon juice

1 garlic clove, crushed

1 teaspoon dried oregano

12 cherry tomatoes, halved

1 cucumber, chopped

1⅓ cups feta cheese, crumbled with a fork

½ red onion, thinly sliced

8 Kalamata olives, pitted and sliced

leaves from a sprig of mint, finely chopped

sea salt and freshly ground black pepper

First make the dressing. Place the olive oil, lemon juice, crushed garlic, and dried oregano in a small bowl, season with salt and pepper, and whisk to combine.

Put the remaining ingredients in a large mixing bowl and pour the dressing over them. Toss well and serve.

SICILIAN HUMMUS

Serves 4

14-oz can chickpeas, rinsed and
drained
about 30 basil leaves
1 garlic clove, crushed
$\frac{1}{2}$ cup almonds
$\frac{1}{2}$ cup pine nuts
zest and juice of 1 lemon
$\frac{3}{4}$ cup olive oil

Put the chickpeas in a food
processor and add the remaining
ingredients. Blend to give a
smooth consistency. The hummus
will last in the fridge for
up to 5 days.

TOMATO SALSA

Serves 4

4 very ripe tomatoes, finely chopped
1 small red onion, finely chopped
2 tablespoons finely chopped fresh
cilantro
1 tablespoon extra virgin olive
oil
1 teaspoon balsamic vinegar
sea salt and freshly ground black
pepper

Put the tomatoes, onion,
cilantro, oil, and vinegar in a
bowl and mix together. Season
to taste with salt and pepper.

TZATZIKI

Serves 4

$1\frac{1}{4}$ cups plain yogurt
$\frac{1}{2}$ cucumber, grated
$\frac{1}{2}$ red onion, finely diced
1 tablespoon finely chopped dill
1 tablespoon finely chopped mint

Place all of the ingredients in
a bowl and stir to combine.

Serves 4

2 sprigs of rosemary, chopped
2 garlic cloves, crushed
1 red chile, finely chopped
$\frac{1}{2}$ cup olive oil
8 lamb chops
sea salt and freshly ground black pepper

BBQ'ED TUSCAN MARINATED LAMB CHOPS

I first discovered this fabulous marinade at a wedding in Tuscany. I squeezed the recipe out of the cook, now I use it to marinate lamb chops, chicken fillets, and meaty fish.

Put the rosemary, garlic, and chile in a bowl and cover with the olive oil. Season with salt and pepper and stir well.

Put the lamb chops in a larger bowl, pour the marinade over, and rub the mixture into the meat. Cover and leave to marinate in the fridge for an hour or more if there is time.

Cook on a hot grill for 3 minutes on each side or for longer if you prefer the meat well done. Delicious served with my Tzatziki (see page 166).

MINI GOURMET BURGERS

I do love a good burger. These mini burgers are great
for a barbecue, but if you like yours larger just shape
to the desired size. If you are making ahead I would do
it the day before, any longer will affect the taste.

Makes 12

1½ lb ground beef
1 red onion, finely chopped
1 tablespoon ketchup
1 teaspoon mustard
1 teaspoon finely chopped
thyme
⅔ cup fresh breadcrumbs
12 mini sesame burger buns
sea salt and freshly ground
black pepper

For the toppings

cheese
lettuce
sliced tomatoes
pickles
red onion rings
mayonnaise

Mix the beef with the red onion, ketchup,
mustard, thyme, and breadcrumbs and season
with salt and pepper. Mix with your hands and
shape into 12 mini burgers. Cook on a hot
barbecue grill for 3-4 minutes on each side.

About a minute before the burger is cooked
put a slice of cheese on top, if you like.
Sandwich the burgers between the burger buns
with whatever toppings you like and secure
with toothpicks.

SPICY LAMB KOFTAS WITH TOMATO SALSA AND TZATZIKI

I love lamb koftas along with a chilled beer on a summer evening. They will set better if you leave them overnight in the fridge. I always try and get the trimmed neck of lamb but good-quality ground lamb works well too.

Serves 4

1 lb ground lamb
1 tablespoon ground cumin
1 teaspoon ground cinnamon
1 red chile, finely chopped
2 tablespoons finely chopped fresh cilantro
2 garlic cloves, crushed
1/2 red onion, finely chopped

To serve

Tzatziki and Salsa (see page 166)
4 flour tortilla wraps
salad leaves

To make the lamb koftas, put all the ingredients into a bowl and mix well. Shape into 16 balls (each about the size of a golf ball), cover with plastic wrap, and place in the fridge to set for 1 hour.

Heat the grill or broiler to medium. (Alternatively set a frying pan over medium heat and add 1 tablespoon of olive oil.) Brown the koftas on all sides then allow to cook for a further 6-8 minutes.

While the lamb is cooking make the salsa and tzatziki (see page 166).

You can serve the lamb koftas on large skewers (four koftas per person) on a bed of salad leaves with the salsa and tatziki. Alternatively, you could serve them on flour tortilla wraps, with salsa, tatziki, and shredded salad leaves, such as romaine lettuce.

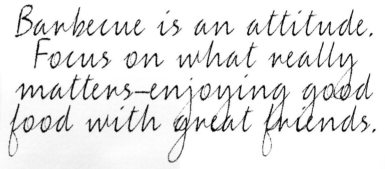

Barbecue is an attitude. Focus on what really matters—enjoying good food with great friends.

MARGARITA

Besides an Old Fashioned, this is my favorite cocktail.
Make sure you chill your glasses in the freezer for
30 minutes before serving.

Makes 1

salt, for rimming the
glass
lots of ice
½ cup tequila
⅓ cup freshly squeezed
lime juice
1 tablespoon Cointreau

Put the salt in a shallow dish. Moisten the rim of a
glass with a damp paper towel and dip it in the salt.

Fill the glass with ice. Add the tequila, lime juice,
and Cointreau and stir a few times until chilled.
Serve immediately.

Serves 4

$1/2$ cup maple syrup
1 teaspoon Dijon mustard
4 tablespoon butter,
melted
4 corn on the cob
salt and black pepper

MAPLE GLAZED GRILLED CORN ON THE COB

Grilled corn on the cob is delicious with just a smear of butter and ground pepper, but add my maple glaze to the mix and you've got the sweetest thing.

Put the maple syrup, mustard, and butter in a bowl and whisk to combine.

Brush the corn on the cob with the glaze and cook on a hot grill for about 20 minutes, turning every few minutes.

CELERY, APPLE, AND LEMON SLAW

I bet this salad will become a staple at your barbecues, it adds a lovely lightness to grilled meats. It will last for up to 3 days in the fridge.

Serves 6

1/2 cup mayonnaise

2 teaspoons finely chopped flat-leaf parsley

juice and zest of 1 lemon

1/2 cup freshly grated horseradish

6 large celery stalks, halved and cut into strips

4 red apples, cored and cut into strips

1 carrot, halved and cut into strips

sea salt and freshly ground black pepper

Toss all the ingredients together in a large serving bowl and season to taste with salt and pepper. Leave to marinate for an hour before serving.

BARBECUED CHICKEN BURGER

I think fast food joints have done the poor chicken burger no justice. When homemade using good quality chicken, and sandwiched in delicious fresh ciabatta rolls they are sublime!

Makes 4

1^1/$_3$ lb ground chicken meat
1^3/$_4$ cups fine breadcrumbs
1 onion, finely diced
1 teaspoon Dijon mustard
1 tablespoon lemon juice
4 burger buns
4 slices of Fontina cheese
sea salt and freshly ground
black pepper

To garnish (optional)

sliced tomato
sliced red onion
lettuce
mayonnaise
Dijon mustard
pickles

In a large bowl combine the chicken, breadcrumbs, onion, mustard, and lemon juice. Season to taste with salt and pepper. Shape into 4 equal patties, each about 3 oz, cover and place in the fridge. Refrigerate for about 1 hour.

Grill the chicken burgers on a hot barbecue grill for 4-5 minutes on each side. Put the cheese on top for the last minute to melt.

Slice and lightly toast the burger buns, put the patties in the buns, and garnish as liked.

Mini Rosemary
Foccacias

AUGUST

SOUTH OF FRANCE

When I lived in Italy we would drive from Turin down the Côte D'Azur to St. Tropez. Sunroof down, scarf tightly tied, and huge film-star glasses. It has to be one of the most beautiful drives in the world. Rocky, mountainous coast, cobalt blue sea, and drenched in sunshine 300 days a year. For my friend, the drive was the main event. For me, the main attraction was and always will be the food.

The produce is sundrenched and vividly colored, just like the land it comes from. The herbs are plentiful and so aromatic; rosemary, marjoram, tarragon, thyme, and basil. While you may be aware of the fantastic seafood here and the abundance of vegetables, you might be surprised to know the area also produces excellent olives, olive oil, and lemons. The region is famous for pistou and passtis. Pistou is a sauce of basil, garlic, and olive oil which is often dropped in soups. Pastis is a yellowy, licorice-flavored drink that old men, and sometimes myself, sit and drink in bars. Don't get them mixed up.

This is the kind of food I thrive on. It's so fresh and flavorful. Grilled fish, straight from the sea, and beautiful, colorful, crisp salads with a light olive oil and lemon dressing. With the vitamin D from the sun and all the goodness of the food, I just feel myself getting healthier with every mouthful. Even the tarte au citrone is doing me good, surely?!

ROASTED TOMATO AND BASIL SOUP WITH PARMESAN TOASTS

This soup is similar to an Italian bruschetta topping, in fact that's how I came up with this recipe. I made too much topping and so I turned it into a soup!

Serves 4

1³/₄ lb cherry or plum tomatoes, cut in half

2 garlic cloves, crushed

1 red onion, cut into large chunks

¹/₂ cup olive oil

1 tablespoon balsamic vinegar

10 basil leaves, torn

2 cups hot chicken or vegetable stock

4 slices of baguette

³/₄ cup grated Parmesan cheese

sea salt and freshly ground black pepper

Preheat the oven to 325°F.

Put the tomatoes, garlic, and onion in a large bowl, pour in the olive oil and vinegar. Season with salt and pepper. Using clean hands, massage the ingredients together for 2 minutes so that the flavors come together. Transfer to a roasting pan and cook in the oven for 20 minutes.

Put the tomatoes, garlic, and onion into a saucepan. Add the basil and stock, set over low heat, and allow to simmer for 15 minutes.

Meanwhile, cover the baguette slices with grated Parmesan and cook in the oven until the cheese has melted. Top each soup bowl with a slice of toast. This soup is also delicious with mini rosemary focaccia (see page 192).

CAMEMBERT AND TOMATO TART

This is a classic dish in good French cafés and I hope it will become a classic in your kitchen too. Try to make the time to chill the pastry for an hour before you bake as this will make the pastry flakier.

Serves 6

For the pastry

1³/₄ cups all-purpose flour

7 tablespoons unsalted butter, cut into small cubes

2 tablespoons water

pinch of salt

For the filling

³/₄ cup Gruyère cheese, grated

1 tablespoon Dijon mustard

1 tablespoon chopped thyme leaves

1 garlic clove, crushed

³/₄ cup camembert cheese, cut into thin strips

10 cherry tomatoes, halved

sea salt and freshly ground black pepper

Make the pastry. Put the butter, flour, and salt in a food processor and blend until the mixture resembles fine breadcrumbs. Pour in the water and mix again until the dough starts to come together, adding more water if necessary.

Put the pastry onto a lightly floured surface, gather together until smooth, then roll out and line a 9 × 1-in loose-bottom fluted tart pan. Trim the edges and press the pastry into flutes. Prick the base with a fork; cover with aluminum foil.

Pour baking beans on top of the foil and blind bake the pastry in the oven for 15 minutes. Remove and allow to cool.

Make the filling. In a bowl mix together the Gruyère, mustard, thyme, garlic, and season with salt and pepper. Pour the mixture into the pastry case, spreading it out evenly with the back of a spoon. Arrange the strips of camembert and halved tomatoes on top and bake in the oven for 35 minutes. Serve warm.

Serves 4

14 oz watermelon, chopped and seeds removed
14 oz plum tomatoes, chopped
1 large cucumber, diced
1 scallion, finely sliced
2 tablespoons extra virgin olive oil
1 tablespoon balsamic vinegar
1 cup feta cheese, crumbled
1 teaspoon dried oregano
sea salt and freshly ground black pepper

SUMMER WATERMELON, FETA, AND MINT SALAD

This is so fresh and bursting with summer flavors.
I sometimes replace the watermelon with cantaloupe,
or add prosciutto and replace the feta with
soft goat cheese.

Put the watermelon, tomatoes, cucumber, and scallion
in a large serving bowl.

Pour over the oil and balsamic vinegar and season with
salt and pepper. Sprinkle the oregano over and mix
well. Crumble the feta over the salad and serve.

SEARED TUNA NIÇOISE SALAD

Please don't be tempted to cook the tuna for longer than one minute on each side, it's too beautiful to be overcooked. This was on the summer menu at Clodagh's Kitchen Restaurant and turned out to be our 2nd best seller!

Serves 2

1 egg, hardboiled and shelled

4 new potatoes, scrubbed, cooked, and halved

12 green beans, cooked

7 oz salad leaves

2 tomatoes, quartered

1/4 cup French dressing

12 black olives

2 fresh tuna steaks

1/8 cup olive oil

sea salt and freshly ground black pepper

Cut the egg into quarters and put in a mixing bowl with the potatoes, green beans, salad leaves, and tomatoes. Pour in the French dressing and toss well. Divide between two plates and sprinkle the olives on top.

Season the tuna steaks with salt and pepper. Put a frying pan over high heat, add the oil, and sear the tuna on both sides for 1 minute. Take care that you do not cook the tuna for longer than 1 minute on each side or it will taste like chicken. Put a tuna steak onto each plate and serve.

PAN-ROASTED JOHN DORY WITH MINTED BEURRE BLANC

John Dory is one of my favorite fish, grilled or roasted.
I particularly love to serve it with my minted beurre
blanc and some spinach and new potatoes.

Serves 4

2 tablespoons butter
8 small fillets of John Dory
juice of 1 lemon
sea salt and freshly ground
black pepper

For the beurre blanc

2 shallots, finely sliced
2 tablespoons white wine vinegar
6 tablespoons Muscadet
2 tablespoons heavy cream
10 tablespoons unsalted butter, diced
juice of 1 lemon
1 tablespoon chopped mint leaves

To make the beurre blanc, place the shallots, vinegar, and wine in
a pan and reduce until there is almost no liquid left. Stir in the
cream and heat gently. Whisk in the butter a little at a time, never
allowing the sauce to boil. Season with lemon juice and a little salt
and black pepper and stir in the fresh mint.

Now cook the John Dory. Place a frying pan over medium heat and
melt the butter. Once the butter is melted, place the fish in the pan
skin-side down and season with salt and pepper. Leave to cook for
3 minutes, then turn and cook for another 4 minutes. Squeeze the juice
of 1 lemon over the fish once you have turned it and chop up the lemon
skin and tuck around the dish to add more flavor.

Serve the fish with a drizzle of the minted beurre blanc, buttered
spinach, and new potatoes.

MINI ROSEMARY FOCCACIAS

Once you get the hang of the method there are endless variations you can make, such as sun-dried tomatoes and basil, olive and oregano, or caramelized red onion and feta.

Makes 4

1 teaspoon fresh yeast
1 teaspoon sugar
1/3 cup warm water
1 cup bread flour
1 teaspoon table salt
olive oil
sea salt, for sprinkling
1 tablespoon finely chopped rosemary

Preheat the oven to 400°F. Line a baking sheet with parchment paper.

Put the yeast and sugar in a small bowl and, using the back of a teaspoon, rub the sugar into the yeast until it turns to liquid. Whisk in the water and continue to whisk for about 2 minutes or until you get a frothy top.

Put the flour in a large bowl and stir in the salt. Make a well in the center and use a wooden spoon to stir in the liquid.

Lightly oil your working surface and place the dough on it. Knead it about 20 times until you have a soft dough. Return it to the bowl and, using your hands, cover it with oil. Cover the bowl with a kitchen towel and put it in a warm place (such as a pantry). After 1 hour turn it back onto an oiled surface and knead again 20 times, returning it to the pantry for another hour.

Turn the dough onto an oiled surface again and cut it into four balls. Oil a wooden rolling pin and roll the balls into small loaves, 4-5 in across. Put them on the baking sheet and use your fingers to make little indentations over the surface. Sprinkle over the finely chopped rosemary and sea salt and cook in the oven for 20 minutes.

OLIVE CRISP BREADS

This is my stand-by bread recipe when I have people coming for dinner. I love placing them on my guests' napkins as they look so colorful.

Makes 8

½ cup warm water

1 teaspoon dry active yeast

1⅔ cups all-purpose flour

2 tablespoons olive oil

3½ oz Kalamata olives, pitted and finely chopped

sea salt

Preheat the oven to 350°F. Line two baking sheets with parchment paper.

Pour the water in a bowl and sprinkle in the yeast. Whisk well and allow the yeast to foam, which should take about 5 minutes.

Sift the flour into a large bowl and make a well in the center. Pour in two-thirds of the yeast mixture and add the oil and a sprinkle of sea salt. Stir together until a dough forms, adding more of the yeast mixture if needed. The dough should be moist but not sticky.

Put the dough onto a floured surface and knead for 10 minutes. Transfer to an oiled bowl, cover with a kitchen towel or plastic wrap, and put in a warm, dry place, such as a pantry, for an hour.

Divide the dough into eight pieces and on a lightly floured surface, roll out each piece to about 9 × 4 in. Transfer to the baking sheet, brush with olive oil, and sprinkle the finely chopped olives on top, using the back of a spoon to push the olives gently into the dough. Bake in the oven for 15 minutes or until crisp and golden. Leave to cool on wire racks before serving.

VARIATIONS

There are so many variations that can be made with the crisp breads. Try any of the following combinations:
• Finely chopped pine nuts.
• Rosemary and sea salt.
• Finely chopped sun-dried tomatoes and dried oregano.

HOMEMADE PIZZA

I make fresh pizza for two reasons; firstly because it tastes so good, and second, at the risk of sounding hippy dippy, I find it therapeutic. Use my fresh tomato pizza base and then top with whatever your heart or tummy desires!

Makes 2 x12in pizzas

¹/₆ oz fresh yeast
1 teaspoon superfine sugar
¹/₄ cup warm water
2¹/₂ cups bread flour
1 teaspoon salt
1 tablespoon olive oil, plus extra
for brushing

Preheat the oven to 450°F.

Put the yeast and sugar in a small bowl and use the back of a teaspoon to rub the sugar into the yeast until it turns to liquid. Whisk in the warm water and continue to whisk for about 2 minutes or until frothy.

Sift the flour into a large bowl and mix in the salt. Make a well in the center of the flour and pour in two-thirds of the yeast into the well of the flour and mix together to give a soft, but not sticky, dough. Add the olive oil and mix well, add extra oil to the dough if needed.

Take the dough out of the bowl. Knead it on a lightly floured worktop for 10 minutes or until it feels smooth and slightly springy. (If you do this in a food mixer with the dough hook it takes half the time.) Let the dough relax for a few minutes.

Shape the dough into two equal balls. Lightly brush the balls with oil, cover, and leave to proof in a warm place, such as a pantry, for 1 hour.

Put a flat sheet or an upside down baking sheet in the oven. (It's easier to slide the pizza on and off if the surface does not have a lip.) On a lightly floured work surface roll out each ball of dough to a circle about 12 in across.

Put a pizza base on a second, cool, upside-down floured tray, spread with Roasted Tomato, Basil, and Olive Sauce (see page 193) and sprinkle with your chosen toppings.

Slide the pizza off the cool tray onto the hot tray in the center of the oven and cook for 5-10 minutes, depending on the heat of the oven and the thickness of the pizza, until the pizza is golden underneath and bubbling on top.

ROASTED TOMATO, BASIL, AND OLIVE SAUCE

This is one of my classic recipes that I use over and over again. You are going to love it, I know you will. Excuse me for sounding confident but it is a great recipe!

Serves 4 for pasta or enough for 2 pizza bases (see page 194)

1¼ cups ripe plum tomatoes, halved

1 onion, finely chopped

2 garlic cloves, crushed

20 black olives, pitted and halved

20 basil leaves

2 tablespoons olive oil

sea salt and freshly ground black pepper

Preheat the oven to 350°F.

Put the tomatoes, cut side up, in a roasting pan. Sprinkle over the onion, garlic, olives, basil, and oil and season with salt and pepper. Cook in the oven for 15 minutes or until the tomatoes have roasted.

When the tomatoes are cooked, transfer the contents of the roasting pan to a food processor and blend to make a smooth sauce.

SPINACH, RICOTTA, AND TOMATO CALZONE

Oooohhh calzones, I love you too much! Really I think I love them more than pizza. I think of them as the Italian pie. You can add pancetta or mushrooms to this recipe too.

Makes 2 calzones

pizza dough (see page 194)

1 tablespoon olive oil, plus extra for brushing

7 oz baby spinach

1 garlic clove, crushed

1/2 cup tomato sauce

2/3 cup ricotta

3/4 cup Parmesan cheese, grated

sea salt and freshly ground black pepper

Preheat the oven to 425°F. Flour a baking sheet.

Make the pizza dough and roll out two circles, each about 12 in across.

Make the filling. Heat the oil in a hot frying pan, add the spinach and toss it briefly in the oil. Add the garlic and continue to cook until the spinach is wilted. Stir in the tomato sauce, ricotta, and Parmesan and season with salt and pepper. Remove from the heat and allow to cool. Take care that the filling isn't too runny, or it will burst through the dough when you cook the calzones. You can thicken with some flour or cornstarch if the filling seems too runny.

Divide the filling evenly between the pizza bases and spread it out. Carefully lift the far edge of the dough circle and pull it over the filling toward you. You should be aiming to fold it in half so that it resembles a large turnover. Brush the edges with olive oil and crimp them so that none of the filling can spill out. Cut a few slashes in the dough. Put the calzones side by side on the baking sheet (use two if necessary). You could also use a pizza stone or granite slab. Cook at the bottom of the oven for 10-15 minutes or until the dough is puffed up and golden on top and the filling is hot.

LEMON DRIZZLE CAKE

This is how a lemon drizzle cake should be; light, fluffy, zesty, and made sweet by the drizzle. It will last about 5 days in an airtight container.

Serves 8-10
For the cake

2 sticks butter, softened

1¼ cups superfine sugar

3 eggs

1¾ cups self-rising flour, sifted

2 teaspoon baking powder, sifted

zest of 2 lemons, plus extra to decorate

juice of 1 lemon

2 tablespoons milk

lemon slices, to decorate

For the drizzle

juice of 2 lemons

1¾ cups confectioners' sugar

Preheat the oven to 350°F. Grease an 8-9 in round cake pan and line the base with parchment paper.

Put the butter in a large mixing bowl with the sugar and beat together with a whisk until light and fluffy.

Slowly beat in the eggs, one at a time. When the eggs are fully incorporated add the milk, then fold in the flour, baking powder, and lemon zest. Pour the cake mixture into the pan and tap the sides to release any air bubbles. Bake in the oven for 35-40 minutes or until the cake is a light golden brown. Check by inserting a skewer into the center of the cake; if it comes out clean the cake is cooked.

While the cake is still hot and still in the pan prick it with a skewer or toothpick and pour over the lemon juice. Leave the cake in the pan to cool.

Make the drizzle. Mix the lemon juice, a little at a time, into the confectioners' sugar to make a smooth paste. Remove the cake from the pan and smooth the icing over the top. Decorate with slices of lemon and extra lemon zest.

HOMEMADE STRAWBERRY ICE CREAM

If you don't have an ice cream maker, freeze once the mixture is made and remove every 30 minutes, whisk, and return to the freezer again.

Serves 8

4 egg yolks
$^2/_3$ cup superfine sugar
$^2/_3$ cup milk
2 cups heavy cream
vanilla pod, or few drops vanilla extract
1 lb strawberries, hulled and roughly chopped

Put the egg yolks in a large bowl and add $^1/_3$ cup superfine sugar. Whisk until light, fluffy, and pale in color.

Put the milk, half the cream, and vanilla seeds or extract in a saucepan and bring to a boil. Watch the pan carefully to make sure it does not overflow. Pour the boiling milk mixture over the whisked egg yolks, whisking all the time to make sure that the eggs do not cook or scramble. Add the remainder of the cream into the bowl and stir. Leave to cool.

In another bowl mix the strawberries with the remaining superfine sugar. Mash the strawberries with a fork until they make a thick sauce. Add to the cooled egg mixture and stir well.

Put the mixture into a clean bowl or container and transfer to the freezer.

After 30 minutes take the bowl from the freezer and whisk to remove any crystals that have formed. Return to the freezer and repeat the whisking process until the ice cream is set. Alternatively, if you have an ice-cream maker, churn the ice cream, transfer it to a container, and freeze until it is ready to eat.

EASY SUMMER ICE CREAM CAKE

I sometimes freeze this in a round cake pan so it looks like a proper cake and then sprinkle chocolates curls all over. It will be one of the quickest cakes you ever make.

Serves 6

1¼ cups whipping cream
8 x 3-in meringue shells
11 oz summer berries
2 teaspoons superfine sugar
½ teaspoon vanilla extract
1 teaspoon mint leaves, finely chopped

Line a 1 lb loaf or cake pan with plastic wrap.

Whip the cream in a bowl. Break up the meringue shells. In a separate bowl use a fork to mash the summer berries with the sugar.

Fold the mashed berries, vanilla extract, and mint into the whipped cream. Stir in the crushed meringues.

Pour the berry and meringue mixture into the cake pan, cover with more plastic wrap, and put in the freezer for 2-3 hours or until frozen.

Take the cake from the freezer just before serving. Remove the plastic wrap from the top, turn the pan over onto a plate or board and remove the rest of the plastic wrap. Serve the cake in slices.

Creamy Walnut
and Cilantro
Pesto

SEPTEMBER

SEPTEMBER PRESERVING PARTY!

Last autumn I had an abundance of gorgeous harvest produce. I had a crate of plump, peppery-smelling tomatoes from a friend's garden, baskets of native Irish apples, a tub of blackberries I picked with my nieces, and armfuls of my homegrown arugula that needed using immediately. Now I know preserving is important and a great way of passing on granny skills but I just wasn't feeling very motivated. Then I had an idea—why not make a necessary and important task into a fun day event for friends? A Preserving Party.

Organization was minimal. I sent a recipe out to each of four friends. On the day, I divided the big island in the center of my kitchen into sections, each with its own cutting board and recipe taped on the work surface next to it. I made a big bowl of pasta for lunch and bought in a few bottles of wine. On the morning I sterilized jars and got the labels ready. And that was it.

As soon as my friends arrived we got started, chopping, chatting, and cooking. The smells were tantalizing, a cross between a souk and a Christmas market. When you're having that much fun you're not aware of how hard you're working. We were astonished when the jars were all filled by lunchtime. Over pasta we kept glancing over at our handiwork with that deep satisfaction you get when you've been really industrious.

At the end of the day we had a sampling session. I brought crackers, cheese, and some pâté to accompany the tomato chutney, walnut and arugula pesto, berry jam, and vanilla and fig compote. I ran out of adjectives and just started groaning with pleasure. Everyone went home not just with a box full of jars for their pantries but a real sense of having spent precious, stolen moments together. We didn't just laugh a lot, we learned a lot. I know it will become an annual tradition and that the five of us will be having preserving parties in our eighties and I can't wait!

STEPS AND TIPS ON PRESERVING

How to test if your jam is cooked

- Place a saucer in a freezer.
- Place a teaspoon of jam on the chilled saucer.
- Drag your finger over the jam.
- If the jam wrinkles then it has set.

How to sterilize your jars

- Preheat the oven to 350°F.
- Thoroughly wash the jars and lids and place them, upside down, on a baking sheet lined with parchment paper.
- Put the jars and lids in the oven for 20 minutes. Remove from the oven and allow to cool.

Tips on preserving

- Only fill each jar to within 2 in of the top.
- If you want to reduce the amount of sugar you use when making jam, substitute half the recommended quantity with honey.
- If the preserve is cooled it should be spooned into a cooled sterilized jar; if the preserve is warm it should be spooned into a warmed sterilized jar.
- When you are bottling nonliquid foods it's important to remove any trapped air bubbles from the top of the jar. Skim the top of the preserve with a knife.

Makes 6 x 8oz jars

1 lb blackberries
1 lb cooking apples,
peeled, cored, and chopped
½ cup water
juice of 1 small lemon
2¼ lb sugar

BLACKBERRY AND APPLE JAM

I have the most wonderful memories of picking
blackberries with my siblings as a child, and taking
our treasured berries back to our mum who would make
blackberry and apple jam. That memory is so precious
to me and nothing will keep me from making this
jam every year.

Put the blackberries, apples, water, and
lemon juice into a large saucepan or
preserving pan. Set the pan over medium heat
and bring to a boil. Reduce the heat and
simmer for 10 minutes.

Stir in the sugar and bring the jam back to a
boil. Continue to boil for 5 minutes, stirring
until all the sugar has dissolved.

Spoon into sterilized jars (see page 204).

VARIATIONS

Strawberry and Vanilla Jam:
Follow recipe left, omitting
the blackberries and apples
and replacing with 2¼ lb
fresh hulled and quartered
strawberries and the seeds
from 1 vanilla pod.

Blueberry Jam:
Follow recipe left, omitting
the blackberries and apples
and replacing with 2¼ lb
fresh blueberries left whole.

FIG JAM

I make fig jam for one thing and that's to eat with aged hard or smoky cheeses, like Pecorino or Coolea; it's a little piece of heaven for me, along with a glass of Côtes du Rhône.

Makes 3 x 8oz jars

²/₃ cup balsamic vinegar
³/₄ cup red wine vinegar
2³/₄ cups brown sugar
zest and juice of
1 lemon
1 red onion, diced
1 teaspoon mustard seeds
2-in piece of fresh
ginger, peeled and
grated
1 teaspoon allspice
1 cinnamon stick
2¹/₄ lb (13) fresh figs
sea salt and freshly
ground black pepper

Put a large saucepan or preserving pan over medium heat and add the vinegars, sugar, lemon zest, and juice, onion, mustard seeds, ginger, allspice, and cinnamon stick. Season to taste with salt and pepper. Stir well and bring to a boil. Reduce the heat and simmer for another 15 minutes or until a thick syrup has formed.

Remove the stems from the figs and cut them in half. Stir them into the thick syrup and continue to simmer for another 20 minutes.

Once the mixture has cooled spoon it into sterilized jars (see page 204).

Makes 6 x 8oz jars
$2^1/_4$ lb (5 large) oranges
1 quart water
juice of 2 lemons
$2^1/_4$ lb sugar

OLD FASHIONED MARMALADE

Homemade marmalade is delicious smothered over toast with a cup of tea. Is there anything better on a September morning? In September in Italy the markets would be stacked with oranges from Sicily.

Cut the oranges into quarters. Using a sharp knife, carefully cut the flesh away from the rind, taking care to leave all the pith behind. Cut the flesh into thin slices and place them in a bowl.

Use a sharp fruit knife or small knife to scrape off and discard all the membrane and pith from the rind. Cut the rind into thin slivers and put them in a saucepan with the water. Bring to a boil, reduce the heat to a simmer, and cook for about 2 hours or until the rinds are tender.

Add the lemon juice to the orange flesh in the bowl and mix. Put the orange flesh in the center of a square of cheesecloth and gather the sides together like a bag. Tie it at the top. Fasten the bag to the handle of a saucepan and allow the bag to hang inside the pan to collect all the juice. Leave it to drain for a couple of hours.

Squeeze any remaining juices from the cheesecloth bag into the saucepan and discard the bag and its contents. Stir in the sugar and orange rind. Put the saucepan over low heat and cook, stirring occasionally, for about 15 minutes or until all the sugar has dissolved.

Allow the orange mixture to sit for 10 minutes off the heat, then spoon it into warmed sterilized jars (see page 204). Leave to cool completely and then cover with a lid.

CREAMY WALNUT AND CILANTRO PESTO

Delicious tossed in pasta, drizzled over soft cheeses,
or as a dip. I sometimes add a little feta into the mix
for a salty version that works well with pasta.

Serves 4

7 cups fresh cilantro
3/4 cup extra virgin olive oil
1/2 cup walnuts
2 garlic cloves
1/2 cup Parmesan cheese,
grated
a pinch of sea salt

Put all the ingredients in a food processor and
blend to give a smooth/coarse texture.

END OF SUMMER TOMATO CHUTNEY

Opening that end of summer burst of flavors in October to
spread over a melted cheese toastie is just heaven. The
chutney will keep for 3 months in a sterilized jar.

Makes about 6½lb kg

4½ lb ripe tomatoes
2-in piece of fresh ginger,
peeled and grated
1 lb apples
1⅓ cups raisins
2 onions, finely diced
½ teaspoon paprika
1 teaspoon chili powder
2 teaspoons salt
3½ cups brown sugar
2½ cups cider vinegar

Peel the tomatoes. Cut a cross at the top of
each one, put them into a large bowl of boiling
water for 5 minutes or until the skins start to
crack (this will depend on how ripe the tomatoes
are). Transfer to a bowl of cold water and
remove the skins.

Put the tomatoes and ginger in a food processor
and blend until smooth.

Set a large saucepan or preserving pan over
medium heat and add the blended tomatoes and
ginger. Stir in the remaining ingredients.
Bring to a boil, reduce the heat, and simmer
for about 40 minutes or until the chutney has
begun to thicken.

Cool and spoon into sterilized jars (see
page 204).

Makes 12 x 8oz jars

4$\frac{1}{2}$ lb cooking apples,
peeled, quartered,
and cored
2 onions
4 tablespoons butter
3$\frac{1}{2}$ cups brown sugar
20 cloves
1 tablespoon chili powder
1 tablespoon turmeric
4-in piece of fresh
ginger, peeled and grated
1$\frac{2}{3}$ cups cider vinegar
sea salt and freshly
ground black pepper

OUR HOUSE CHUTNEY

This really is the best preserve that I
have made, it lasts for about 3 months
and is even better if left to age for at
least 1 week before you eat.

Chop the apples into small chunks and dice the onions.

Set a large saucepan or preserving pan over low heat and
melt the butter. Add the apples and onions, then add
the sugar, cloves, chili powder, turmeric, ginger, and
cider vinegar. Season to taste with salt and pepper
and mix well.

Cover the saucepan, increase the heat, and bring to a
boil. Reduce the heat and leave to simmer over medium
heat for 20 minutes, stirring every 5 minutes.

Take off the saucepan lid, turn down the heat, and leave
to cook for 30 minutes until the apple has broken down
and the chutney has turned a rich, golden brown color.
Use the back of a wooden spoon to crush the apples if
necessary. Take the pan off the heat and allow to cool.
The chutney will thicken more as it cools.

Spoon the cool chutney into sterilized jars (see
page 204).

LUNCHBOXES

Stolen moments are important. Taking back a little time to do
something good for yourself isn't selfish, it's an investment
in your own well-being. It's all too easy to grab a soggy
sandwich at lunchtime and sit at your desk in front of the
computer. With very little planning you could steal back a few
moments to give yourself a real treat.

I have a friend, Tom. When he takes the lid off his packed
lunch he lifts it up, smells it, and smiles. He brings his own
cloth napkin to work and a little knife to slice cold meats,
cheese, or fruits. He is a connoisseur of the lunchbox and
here's what I learned from him:

Find yourself a little pot (the individual catering jars of
jam and mustard are perfect); use this for your chutneys,
pesto, and pickles. If you put them straight into the sandwich
it will be soggy by lunchtime. It doesn't always have to be
bread, mix it up with salads, tortillas, or hearty homemade
soups. And finally, always pack yourself a treat. For Tom that
was something home baked and sweet and the envy of all who
worked with him.

Get away from your desk if you can. Go outside, meet a friend,
and share your packed lunches; sit by the river. Give yourself
the time to enjoy your food. Let's put the pleasure back into
the packed lunch. Here are some of my recipes for the
delicious sandwiches and salads we make at Clodagh's Bakery
in Dublin.

ITALIAN MINESTRONE SOUP

On the piazza where I lived in Turin, there was a fabulous daily market. I would pop down early in the morning and fill my bag with delicious vegetables to make this soup.

Serves 6

2 tablespoons olive oil

1 onion, finely chopped

2 garlic cloves, crushed

1 carrot, finely chopped

1 celery stalk, finely chopped

1 zucchini, finely chopped

3⅓ cups hot vegetable stock

14 oz can chopped tomatoes

14 oz can chickpeas, rinsed and drained

1 teaspoon dried oregano

sea salt and freshly ground black pepper

Put a large saucepan over medium-high heat, pour in the oil, and then stir in the onion and garlic. Cover and allow to cook for 2 minutes.

Stir in the carrot, celery, and zucchini. Cover and leave to cook for another 5 minutes.

Pour in the stock, tomatoes, and chickpeas. Bring to a boil, reduce the heat, and simmer. Stir in the oregano, season with salt and pepper, and continue to simmer for about 10 minutes.

CHICKEN CAESAR WRAP

Creamy, crunchy, and light—the perfect summer lunch.
Try adding a sun-dried tomato salad with lime dressing.

Makes 2 wraps

1 chicken breast
2 tablespoons Caesar dressing
(see page 113)
8 romaine lettuce leaves
2 flour wraps
1 tablespoon pine nuts, toasted
and roughly chopped

For the marinade

juice of ½ lemon
1 garlic clove, crushed
1 tablespoon olive oil
sea salt and freshly ground
black pepper

Preheat the oven to 350°F.

Make the marinade. Put the lemon juice, garlic, and oil in a bowl or sealable freezer bag and season with salt and pepper. Add the chicken, mix well, and leave in the fridge for 30 minutes.

Place a griddle or frying pan over medium heat and sear the chicken for about 3 minutes on each side or until golden in color. Transfer to the oven and cook for 10 minutes. Remove and allow to cool.

Cut the chicken into strips, place in a bowl with the Caesar dressing, and mix well.

Open out the wraps and place the lettuce in the center of each. Add the chicken, sprinkle over the chopped pine nuts, and fold the wraps to close.

Try adding any of the following:

- Sun-dried tomatoes
- Croutons
- Crispy bacon pieces

Makes 2

2 Mini Rosemary Focaccias (see page 192)
extra virgin olive oil
1 ball of fresh buffalo mozzarella, sliced
6 sun-dried tomatoes, roughly chopped
2 slices of prosciutto
6 fresh basil leaves, torn
sea salt and freshly ground black pepper

THE ITALIAN JOB

For the cheese, use mozzarella di buffalo—and,
as September is the best month for tomatoes, I would
use fresh—but once out of season, I'll be
using sun-dried.

Cut the focaccias in half lengthwise and brush
with oil.

Divide the mozzarella and tomatoes between the
focaccias. Add a slice of prosciutto to each
and scatter over the basil. Season with salt
and pepper and close the sandwich.

TUNA MELT

When you're shopping for canned tuna, look for the "sustainably fished" logo. The cucumber adds a gorgeous freshness. You could also toss the filling in salad leaves.

Makes 2

6-oz can tuna, preferably in oil, drained and flaked
1/3 cup mayonnaise
1/2 celery stalk, finely sliced
1/4 red onion, finely sliced
juice of 1/2 lemon
2 demi sourdough baguettes
4 slices of tomato
2 in cucumber, finely diced
2 slices of Swiss cheese
sea salt and freshly ground pepper

Preheat the oven to 400°F.

Put the tuna, mayonnaise, celery, onion, and lemon juice in a bowl. Season with salt and pepper and mix well.

Cut the baguettes in half lengthwise and divide the tuna mixture between them. Put two slices of tomato in each sandwich, followed by a slice of cheese. Close the baguette together.

Cook in the oven for 5-7 minutes.

Alternatively, cook the sandwich in a grill pan or sandwich maker.

MINI 3 BEAN SALAD

Bursting with fiber, this salad will give you that extra "oomph" for your afternoon at work. We serve this on the salad counter in the food court. I try and have a portion 3 times a week—so stock up your pantry with canned pulses!

Makes 10 mini salads

14-oz can cannellini beans, rinsed and drained

14-oz can kidney beans, rinsed and drained

14-oz can chickpeas, rinsed and drained

1 celery stalk, finely sliced

1/2 red onion, finely diced

3 tablespoons finely chopped flat-leaf parsley

1 garlic clove, crushed

1 teaspoon dried oregano

For the vinaigrette:

1/2 cup extra virgin olive oil

1/3 cup cider vinegar

sea salt and freshly ground black pepper

Make the vinaigrette. Whisk together the oil and vinegar and season to taste with salt and pepper.

Put all the ingredients for the salad in a large mixing bowl. Pour the vinaigrette over and mix well. Cover and place in the fridge for an hour before serving.

Makes 5 mini salads

¹/₂ cup of flaked almonds
3¹/₂ cups carrots, chopped
(about 6 large carrots)
²/₃ cup golden raisins
1 tablespoon finely chopped
flat-leaf parsley

For the vinaigrette:

2 tablespoons extra virgin olive oil
5 tablespoons white wine vinegar
sea salt and freshly ground black
pepper

MINI CARROT, RAISIN, AND ALMOND SALAD

Gorgeous alongside a slice of quiche or sandwich and lovely tumbled in with my 3 bean salad. This salad is another staple in my salad bar at Homemade Food Court. Make a big batch and this salad will last up to 4 days in the fridge.

Toast the almonds on a dry baking sheet in the oven at 350°F for 10 minutes or in a dry frying pan until golden brown. Set aside to cool.

Peel the carrots and grate them into a large bowl using the large side of the grater. Mix in the raisins and almonds.

Make the vinaigrette. Whisk together the oil and vinegar and season to taste with salt and pepper.

Pour the vinaigrette over the carrots and mix well. Cover and place in the fridge for an hour.

Add the parsley just before serving.

CHICKEN, AVOCADO, AND SUN-DRIED TOMATO SALAD WITH A LIME DRESSING

The lime dressing in this salad adds a delicious zestiness to the chicken and avocado. Triple the dressing recipe and it will keep in the fridge for up to 2 weeks.

For the Chicken:

juice of ½ lemon
1 garlic clove, crushed
1 tablespoon olive oil
1 skinless chicken breast
sea salt and freshly ground black pepper

For the Salad:

mixed salad leaves
1 avocado, sliced
8 sun-dried tomatoes
16 pumpkin seeds

For the Dressing:

3 tablespoons extra virgin olive oil
juice of 1 lime

Preheat the oven to 350°F.

Put the lemon juice, garlic, and oil in a bowl or sealable freezer bag and season with salt and pepper. Add the chicken to the marinade and mix well. Put in the fridge for 30 minutes.

Put a griddle or frying pan over medium heat and sear the chicken for about 3 minutes on each side or until golden in color. Transfer to the oven for 10 minutes to cook completely. Remove and allow to cool.

Cut the chicken into strips and put them in a bowl. Add the salad leaves, avocado slices, sun-dried tomatoes and pumpkin seeds.

Make the dressing. Whisk together the oil and lime juice and season with salt and pepper. Pour the dressing over the salad and toss to mix.

VERMICELLI NOODLE SALAD WITH ONION AND SESAME DRESSING

This delicious salad makes a fabulous Eastern inspired lunch. The onion and sesame dressing adds a great flavor to the noodles.

Serves 2

2¼ cups mung beans or vermicelli noodles

a handful of seeds (such as pumpkin, sunflower, or sesame)

a splash of soy sauce

1 carrot, finely grated

1 beet, finely grated

½ daikon (Japanese radish), finely grated (or a white cabbage heart)

2 tablespoons finely chopped fresh cilantro

2 tablespoons scallions, finely chopped

For the Onion & Sesame Dressing:

½ large onion or 1 small onion, diced

½ cup soy sauce

½ cup sesame oil

⅓ cup rice vinegar

2 tablespoons superfine sugar

sesame seeds, for sprinkling

Preheat the oven to 350°F.

Make the dressing by putting all the ingredients (except the sesame seeds) in a blender. Mix until smooth, transfer to a bowl, and sprinkle the sesame seeds over the top.

Cook the noodles in boiling water for 2-3 minutes or according to the package instructions. Cool under cold running water and drain well.

Place the seeds on a baking sheet, sprinkle over the soy sauce, and cook in the oven for 5-7 minutes.

Using your hands, gently mix the noodles with all the other ingredients until you're happy with the blend. Sprinkle the warm seeds on top and serve with the sauce on the side.

HEAVENLY CHOCOLATE BROWNIES

You can substitute the walnuts with hazelnuts, or fresh
berries such as raspberries. Make a lovely big tray and
store them in an airtight container and they will last
for up to a week.

Makes 20

2 sticks butter

6½ oz dark chocolate
(70 percent cocoa
solids), chopped

½ cup walnuts, chopped

¾ cup cocoa powder,
sifted

½ cup all-purpose flour,
sifted

1 teaspoon baking
powder, sifted

1¾ cups superfine sugar

4 large eggs

Preheat the oven to 350°F. Line a 10-in square
baking pan with parchment paper.

In a large bowl set over simmering water, melt
the butter and the chocolate. Mix until smooth.
Add the walnuts and stir together.

In a separate bowl mix together the cocoa
powder, flour, baking powder, and sugar. Add
the dry ingredients to the chocolate and nut
mixture and stir together well. Beat the eggs
and stir into to the chocolate mixture to give
a silky consistency.

Pour the brownie mix into the baking sheet and
cook in the oven for about 25 minutes. Brownies
shouldn't be overcooked, so, unlike cakes, you
don't want a skewer to come out clean. The
brownies should be slightly springy on the
outside but still gooey in the middle. Leave to
cool in the pan, then carefully transfer to a
large board and cut into chunky squares.

LEMON AND RASPBERRY MUFFINS

You can make a lot of different variations of this recipe. At my bakery we use this recipe but vary it to make Orange and Blueberry, Banana and Cinnamon, Apple, Raisin, and Raspberry, or Lemon and White Chocolate.

Makes 12

7 tablespoons unsalted butter, melted
1 cup brown sugar
2 eggs
1 cup milk
1 cup all-purpose flour, sifted
2 teaspoon baking powder, sifted
pinch of salt
5 oz fresh raspberries
1 tablespoon grated lemon zest

Preheat the oven to 350°F. Line a 12-hole muffin pan with paper baking cups.

Put the butter in a large mixing bowl with the sugar and whisk together until light and fluffy. Slowly beat in the eggs, a little at a time, followed by the milk. Fold the flour, baking powder, and salt into the mixture.

Gently fold the raspberries and lemon zest into the mixture and spoon the batter into the paper baking cups. Bake in the oven for 20 minutes or until the muffins are a light, golden brown. Check that they are cooked by inserting a skewer into the middle of a muffin; if it comes out clean the muffin is cooked.

Allow to cool for 5 minutes in the pan before transferring to a wire rack to cool.

WHITE CHOCOLATE AND MACADAMIA COOKIES

This is a soft cookie dough that you can wrap in plastic wrap and refrigerate or freeze for whenever you want to use it. Serve with a big glass of cold milk or tuck in your lunchbox for an afternoon treat.

Makes 16

1 stick of butter, softened

¾ cup brown sugar

½ cup superfine sugar

1 egg

1 teaspoon vanilla extract

2 cups all-purpose flour

½ teaspoon baking soda

½ teaspoon baking powder

1¼ cups toasted macadamia nuts, chopped

8 oz white chocolate chips or chopped chocolate

Preheat the oven to 350°F. Line two baking sheets with parchment paper.

Beat together the butter and sugars until light and fluffy. Beat in the egg, a little at a time, and the vanilla extract.

Sift the flour, baking soda, and baking powder into the butter and egg mixture and beat together until the cookie dough comes together. Beat in the nuts and chocolate.

Use your hands to make 16 walnut-sized balls from the dough. Put them on the baking sheets and use the back of a spoon to flatten them into disks about 2 in across. Space the cookies about 3in apart because they will expand during cooking.

Bake in the oven for 15-20 minutes or until they are golden brown in color. Leave to cool on a wire rack.

OCTOBER

Christmas cake

Spiced Butternut
Squash and
Coconut Soup

CHRISTMAS BAKING

The big Christmas Bake was a huge tradition in our house—my granny would bring the recipe for Christmas cake and pudding and Mum would get the ingredients. My sisters, brother, and I would weigh and mix ingredients and cut circles of parchment paper. Each of us would make a wish as we stirred the pudding mix and take turns to lick the bowls. We were having fun but we were also learning treasured family recipes, and picking up valuable skills from Granny and Mum. Those days provided a real sense of continuity between the generations in our family.

With my work I spend a good deal of time talking to people about food. Something that keeps coming up with younger people, the pre-prepared food generation, is that they feel disconnected from these traditions. They loved watching their own mums and grans cook but don't have the confidence to do it themselves, simply because they don't cook much at any other time of year. It worries them that they won't have the skills to pass on to their own kids.

So when I started Christmas Baking classes at my cooking school, I wasn't surprised at the uptake or that most of the class were younger than usual. I was delighted when many of them made a pact to do the same again the following October. I know we can't all be with our families but why not get a group of friends together to start an annual tradition of Christmas baking, take pictures, talk about your memories, about how your mother used to bake, and keep the tradition alive! Every autumn we keep the grand Christmas baking tradition alive in my bakery and the smells waft throughout the kitchens. Oh yes, Christmas isn't too far away now…

CHRISTMAS CAKE

Traditionally Christmas cakes are made at the end of November, but I always make mine in October to allow more time for the flavors to develop.

Makes 1 cake

3 cups currants

1¼ cups raisins

⅓ cup candied cherries

⅓ cup mixed candied peel

4 tablespoons brandy, plus extra for feeding

1¾ cups all-purpose flour

½ teaspoon salt

¼ teaspoon freshly grated nutmeg

½ teaspoon mixed spice

2 sticks unsalted butter

1½ cups brown sugar

4 large eggs

⅓ cup chopped almonds

1 teaspoon molasses

grated zest of 1 lemon

grated zest of 1 orange

¾ cup whole blanched almonds (optional)

The day before you want to bake the cake put the dried fruit, cherries, and mixed peel in a bowl. Mix with the brandy as evenly and thoroughly as possible, then cover the bowl with a clean kitchen towel and leave overnight, or for at least 12 hours so that the fruit absorbs the brandy.

Preheat the oven to 275°F. Grease and line an 8-in round cake pan or a 7-in square pan with parchment paper. Tie a band of brown paper around the outside of the pan for extra protection.

Sift the flour, salt, and spices into a large mixing bowl, lifting it high to give the flour a good airing.

In a separate large bowl, using an electric beater, whisk together the butter and sugar until the mixture is light and fluffy. Beat the eggs in a separate bowl and add them to the creamed mixture a tablespoonful at a time. Keep the beater running until all the eggs are incorporated; if you add the eggs slowly it is less likely that the mixture will curdle.

Fold the flour and spices into the mixture, using gentle, folding movements so that you keep the air in; do not beat the mixture. Fold in the fruit, peel, chopped almonds, molasses, and the grated lemon and orange zests. (The molasses will be easier to measure if you remove the lid and put the jar in a small pan of barely simmering water.)

Use a large kitchen spoon to transfer the mixture into the cake pan, spreading it out evenly with the back of the spoon. If you don't intend to ice the cake lightly drop the whole blanched almonds in circles or squares over the surface.

Cover the top of the cake with a double square of
parchment paper with a 10-in hole in the center to
give extra protection during the long, slow cooking.
Bake the cake on the lowest shelf of the oven for
$4\frac{1}{2}$-$4\frac{3}{4}$ hours. It can sometimes take up to 30-45 minutes
longer than this, but in any case don't look until at
least 4 hours have passed.

Leave the cake to cool in the pan for 30 minutes, then
transfer it to a wire rack to finish cooling. When the cake
is completely cold "feed" it by making small holes in the
top and base of the cake with a toothpick or small skewer
and spoon over a few teaspoons of brandy. Wrap the cake in
a double layer of parchment paper secured with a rubber
band and either wrap it in aluminum foil or store in an
airtight container. If you wish, you can feed it at
intervals until you need to ice or eat it.

MY MUM'S CHRISTMAS PUDDING

Every year my mum makes a Christmas pudding for me and
my siblings, as her mother did before her. I love this
tradition and plum puddings are a lovely gift.

Makes 2

butter, for greasing
$1^3/_4$ cups all-purpose flour
1 teaspoon mixed spice
1 teaspoon grated nutmeg
$^1/_3$ cup slivered almonds
$2^1/_2$ cups dark brown sugar
1 cup shredded shortening
$1^1/_2$ cups golden almonds
$1^1/_2$ cups currants
$1^1/_2$ cups raisins
$1^1/_2$ cups mixed peel
$1^1/_2$ cups dried white
breadcrumbs
6 eggs
5 tablespoons Irish stout
juice of 1 orange
$^1/_2$ cup brandy
$^1/_2$ cup milk

Butter two $2^1/_2$-cup pudding basins.

In a large bowl sift the flour, mixed spice, and
nutmeg. Mix in the almonds, sugar, shortening, dried
fruit, mixed peel, and breadcrumbs. In a separate bowl
combine the eggs, stout, orange juice, brandy, and
milk. Stir the liquid mixture into the dry
ingredients.

Divide the mixture between the pudding basins. For
each pudding cut a round of parchment paper $1^1/_2$ times
the size of the rim of the basin. Grease, then fold a
single pleat in the paper to allow room for the
pudding to expand during cooking. Cover each pudding
with parchment and secure with string.

Place each pudding into a saucepan with water halfway
up the side. Cover and steam for 6 hours or longer.
The longer a pudding cooks, the richer and darker it
becomes. Add boiling water to each pan as required and
don't let the water boil dry.

To store: Remove the parchment
paper rounds and replace with
new ones. Wrap each pudding in
a cloth and store in a cool
dry place until required.

To reheat: Steam each pudding for
2 hours and serve.

Makes 6 lb

12 oz seedless raisins
8 oz golden raisins
8 oz currants
5 oz mixed peel
12 oz brown sugar
1 lb cooking apples, peeled, cored,
and grated
8 oz shredded shortening
grated rind and juice of 2 oranges
grated rind and juice of 2 lemons
2 oz slivered almonds
2 oz chopped pecans
1 tablespoon mixed spice
1 teaspoon grated nutmeg
5 fl oz brandy

CHRISTMAS MINCEMEAT

I know it sounds strange to roast the mincemeat, but this tip, given to me by my sister Mairead, who is a fabulous cook, really does bring out the flavors.

Mix together all the ingredients, except half the brandy, in a large, ovenproof bowl, cover and leave to stand overnight.

Preheat the oven to 225°F.

Cover the bowl with aluminum foil and cook in the oven for about 3 hours. Allow to cool, then mix in the rest of the brandy and transfer to sterilized jars (see page 204).

HALLOWEEN

Halloween is absolutely the time to embrace your inner child or perhaps your inner goth. Just think graveyards, ghosts, ghouls, creepy crawlies, body parts, and lots of blood. Get yourself an icing gun, three or four different food colors (red is essential), a paintbrush, and a sheet of roll out fondant. Any flat cookie serves as the body of a creepy crawly or a ghoul, just paint or ice on gruesome features. Graham crackers make great tombstones. Use your icing gun to apply guests' names.

Licorice sticks are good for spider legs; they are bendy but hold their shape when attached to cookies, cakes, or other sweets. Just add a couple of candy eyes. Gob stoppers make great eyeballs and Snowballs or little Ferrero Rocher are great for attaching ears and tails to. Slightly under set gelatin is perfect for green slime.

For the adults, what about a blood red wine punch? Just drop a dry ice pellet in for that eerie, fog effect. Devils on horseback are always a winner. Go on you devil, tease out some cotton candy cobwebs and dribble some red food coloring from the corner of your mouth.Cue villainous laugh, "Mee, haw, haw, haw."

BLOODTHIRSTY PUNCH

Delight children and adults alike with this ghoulish drink for a spooky occasion. Looks great served in a punch bowl at a party too.

Serves 10

32 oz lemon-lime soda
32 oz cranberry juice
juice of 3-4 limes

Fill a clean dishwashing glove with water, secure the end with a freezer clip or rubber band, and place it in the freezer overnight.

Stir together the soda, cranberry juice, and lime juice, and pour into a punch bowl or large jug.

Remove the hand from the freezer and use scissors to remove the glove. Put the frozen hand in the punch bowl and serve.

5 large egg whites, at
room temperature
½ cup superfine sugar
1 cup confectioners'
sugar
dark chocolate chips,
to decorate

GHOST MERINGUES

These are so much fun to make with children. Super easy
too, I promise you. I used to make them with the kids
that came for my Halloween cooking class.

Preheat the oven to 225°F. Line two baking sheets with nonstick liner or
parchment paper (meringue can stick on aluminum foil).

Put the egg whites into a large, clean mixing bowl (not plastic). Beat them on
medium speed with an electric beater until the mixture resembles a fluffy cloud
and stands up in stiff peaks when the blades are lifted.

Increase the speed of the beater and start to add the superfine sugar, a
teaspoon at a time. Continue beating for 3-4 seconds between each addition.
It's important to add the sugar slowly to prevent the meringue from oozing
later, but don't over-beat. When it is ready the mixture should be thick
and glossy.

Sift one-third of the confectioners' sugar over the mixture, then gently fold
it in with a big metal spoon or rubber spatula. Continue to sift and fold in
the confectioners' sugar, a third at a time. Don't overmix. The mixture should
now look smooth and billowy, almost like a snow drift.

Scoop the mixture into a piping bag with a ¾-in nozzle. Squeeze into
ghostlike shapes about 1in apart. Carefully add the chocolate chip "eyes."
Bake in the oven for 1½ hours so that the meringues are still white but can
be lifted from the parchment without sticking. Turn off the oven, leave the
door ajar, and leave the meringues until cold. The meringues will now keep in
an airtight container for up to 2 weeks or frozen for a month.

SPICED PUMPKIN CAKE

The cake is quite light but the frosting is sinful! Make the base the day before, and then make up the icing the day you are going to eat it.

Makes 1 cake

1$\frac{1}{2}$ sticks unsalted butter, softened

1$\frac{1}{4}$ cups dark brown sugar

1 cup sugar

4 eggs

1 cup pumpkin purée

$\frac{1}{2}$ cup buttermilk

1 teaspoon vanilla extract

2$\frac{1}{2}$ cups flour

2 teaspoons baking powder

1 teaspoon baking soda

1 teaspoon ground cinnamon

$\frac{1}{2}$ teaspoon ground nutmeg

For the Icing:

$\frac{1}{2}$ cup cream cheese

3 tablespoons unsalted butter, softened

$\frac{1}{4}$ cup pumpkin purée

1 teaspoon vanilla extract

1 tablespoon freshly squeezed orange juice

1 teaspoon grated orange zest

3$\frac{1}{3}$ cups confectioners' sugar

Preheat the oven to 350°F. Grease the bases and sides of two 10in cake pans and line the bases with parchment paper.

Put the butter and sugars in a large mixing bowl and use an electric beater to cream them together until light and fluffy. Whisk in the eggs, one at a time, then add the pumpkin purée, buttermilk, and vanilla extract. Combine well.

Sift in the flour, baking powder, baking soda, cinnamon, and nutmeg and combine until smooth. Pour the mixture into the cake pans and tap the sides to release any air bubbles. Bake in the oven for 35-40 minutes or until the cake is a light golden brown. Check by inserting a skewer into the center of the cake; if it comes out clean the cake is cooked. Allow the cakes to cool in the pans and then move to a wire rack.

Meanwhile, make the icing. Beat together the cream cheese, butter, pumpkin purée, vanilla extract, orange juice, and zest with an electric beater until smooth. Add the confectioners' sugar and continue to beat until light and fluffy.

Top one of the cakes with half the icing and put the other cake on top. Cover the top of the cake with the remaining icing.

MARSHMALLOW BRAINS

You can make these the day before you throw a Halloween party as they keep well. Also try adding candy-coated chocolate drops or chocolate chips to the mix.

Makes 10

3 oz popcorn kernels
1 tablespoon vegetable oil, plus extra for shaping
2 tablespoons butter
11 large marshmallows

Line a baking sheet with parchment paper.

Put the popping corn and oil in a large pan set over medium heat. Stir the kernels around the pan to coat in the oil.

When the kernels start to pop, place a lid firmly on top and turn down the heat to low. Cook for about 5 minutes, shaking the pan often to stop the popcorn burning or sticking, until the corn has stopped popping. Pour into a bowl, discarding any unopened kernels.

Heat the butter and marshmallows over low heat until melted. Pour the mixture over the popcorn and mix well until coated. Lightly rub oil over your hands and shape the popcorn into small balls. Put on the baking sheet and leave to set.

FREAKY FINGERS

Candied cherries work the best for this recipe but you could also use chocolate chips for black fingernails.

Makes 20

1/2 cup superfine sugar
7 tablespoons butter
1 egg yolk
1 2/3 cups all-purpose flour
1/2 teaspoon vanilla extract
a pinch of salt
candied cherries, cut into fingernail shapes or strawberry jam

Preheat the oven to 350°F. Line a baking sheet with parchment paper.

Put all the ingredients, except the candied cherries or jam, in a food processor and blend just until a ball of dough forms.

Tear off pieces of dough about the size of a golf ball and use your hands to roll them into finger-size cylinders; you should get about 20 in total.

Place the fingers on the baking sheet, spacing them a little apart because they will spread during baking, and use a knife to make a few cuts, close together, to represent knuckles.

Position a nail-shaped cherry at one tip of each finger or use strawberry jam and bake in the oven for 10-12 minutes just until firm. Leave to cool.

NUTTY TOFFEE APPLES

You can't have a Halloween party without toffee apples.
You can omit the nuts if you if wish, but definitely
not the toffee!

Makes 6 apples

6 small wooden popsicle
sticks

6 eating apples

2 cups sugar

½ cup water

2 tablespoons butter

2 tablespoons corn syrup

4 tablespoons finely
chopped mixed nuts

Line a baking sheet with nonstick parchment paper.
Push the wooden sticks halfway into the apples at the
stalk end.

Dissolve the sugar and water in a thick-bottomed pan
over gentle heat. Add the butter and syrup to the
mixture and bring to a boil. Continue to boil, without
stirring, until the toffee reaches 550°F (use a sugar
thermometer to measure this).

Remove the pan from the heat and gently stir in
the nuts.

Carefully dip each apple into the toffee, making sure
that each one is well coated, and set aside to harden
on the baking sheet.

BAKED CINNAMON AND GOLDEN RAISIN APPLES

My dad used to make these for us when we were growing up. I love them so much, not only because of the memory of him making them but also because they are what October means to me...

Serves 4

4 cooking apples
¾ cup brown sugar
2 teaspoons honey
2 teaspoons ground cinnamon
½ cup golden raisins
16 cloves
2 tablespoons butter

Preheat the oven to 350°F.

Remove the apple cores with a corer and use a teaspoon to enlarge the cavity to double the size. Place the apples in an ovenproof dish.

In a small bowl mix together the sugar, honey, cinnamon, and raisins and fill each apple with the mixture. Pierce each apple with 4 cloves, add a small piece of butter to the top of each apple, and cook in the oven for 20 minutes.

Serve hot with whipped cream.

SPICED BUTTERNUT SQUASH AND COCONUT SOUP

This combination works so well together. If you are not a fan of coconut milk then just replace with vegetable or chicken stock and try adding a little chorizo.

Serves 4

2 tablespoons butter

2¼ lb butternut squash, skinned, seeded, and cut into 1-in pieces

1 teaspoon ground cumin

1 teaspoon garam masala

2 garlic cloves, crushed

1½ cups onions, chopped

3 cups hot vegetable stock

1¼ cups coconut milk

sea salt and freshly ground black pepper

Melt the butter in a heavy-bottomed saucepan, add the squash, spices, garlic, and onions and season with salt and pepper. Cover and leave to simmer, stirring occasionally, for about 15 minutes.

Stir in the stock and coconut milk and bring the soup to a boil. When the squash is tender the soup is ready to be blended using a food processor or immersion blender. Serve hot.

BUTTERNUT SQUASH AND PARMESAN RISOTTO

You need to be patient when making a risotto, adding a little stock at a time, stirring and tasting as you go, but it's so worth the time and effort.

Serves 4

5 tablespoons butter, plus extra for finishing

1 shallot, finely chopped

2 garlic cloves, crushed

1½ cups risotto rice

½ cup dry white wine

2¼ lb butternut squash

3 cups hot vegetable stock

1½ cups grated Parmesan cheese, plus extra for serving

½ cup mascarpone cheese

sea salt and freshly ground black pepper

Melt the butter in a large saucepan, add the shallots and garlic, and cook gently for 3-4 minutes, until softened. Add the rice and stir for a minute to coat the rice in the butter. Pour in the white wine and let it bubble for a few minutes to allow the alcohol to evaporate.

Meanwhile, prepare the butternut squash. Peel the squash, take out all the seeds, and chop the flesh into small cubes. Add the butternut squash to the risotto rice, and stir well.

Every couple of minutes add a ladle of stock to the pan. Stir and allow the rice to absorb the juices. Repeat until all the stock has been absorbed.

When the rice is tender, stir in the Parmesan and mascarpone cheese and season to taste with salt and pepper. Scatter over extra Parmesan before serving.

WILD MUSHROOMS WRAPPED IN PAPPARDELLE AND PANCETTA

This is a more delicate version of the traditional carbonara. If you can't get fresh wild mushrooms then use good-quality dried ones and rehydrate them. You could add a few button mushrooms into the mix, too. Halved and roasted cherry tomatoes and a few torn fresh basil leaves also work well.

Serves 4

5 tablespoons butter
4 oz pancetta, chopped
1 garlic clove, crushed
3 cups wild mushrooms
juice of $\frac{1}{2}$ lemon
1 cup crème fraîche
$\frac{2}{3}$ cup Parmesan cheese, plus extra for serving
1 teaspoon finely chopped sage
$4\frac{1}{3}$ cups pappardelle, cooked al dente
sea salt and freshly ground black pepper

Set a saucepan over medium heat and melt the butter. Add the pancetta and cook for 3 minutes. Stir in the garlic, then the mushrooms, and cook for another 2 minutes.

Add the lemon juice, crème fraîche, Parmesan, and sage to the pan and stir well. Cook for 5 minutes or until the sauce has thickened a little.

Stir in the cooked pasta and combine well. Season to taste with salt and pepper. Serve with plenty of grated Parmesan cheese.

Pappardelle
with Beef
Ragu

Chicken, Tarragon,
and Mushroom Pie

NOVEMBER

MOVIE NIGHTS

What is it with popcorn and crunchy snacks in movie theaters? It's like encouraging teenagers to play *Grand Theft Auto* in church. Years ago I organized picnic baskets, filled with artisan produce, for cinema-goers at the Cork Film Festival. It was so civilized, romantic, and quiet! It was for an event at the Kino cinema, Ireland's only independent art house cinema, now sadly closed. It made me aware of how closely film and food are linked.

Have you noticed how films about food always involve passion and sensuality? Think of the denial and self-gratification in the lavish banquet in *Babette's Feast*; of how the sweetness of the confectionary in *Chocolat* melts the sourness of the bourgeoisie; and how Tilda Swinton is seduced by the sublime food of the chef in *I am Love*.

I've given up on multiplex theaters. It's such a soulless experience. Nowadays I occasionally go to art house or independent theaters, the Irish Film Institute in Dublin is great. But on a cold November evening I am happier to watch movies at home and cook. I think film and food are very natural pleasures to mix. I like to match the food I am making to the world of the film I am watching. Just try it! Curl up with *Cinema Paradiso* and a bowl of Pappardalle; tuck into a spicy curry and watch *Slumdog Millionaire*. Or for the ultimate in romance watch *Casablanca* with couscous and a lamb tagine. This could be the beginning of a beautiful friendship!

SMOKED TROUT AND MUSSEL CHOWDER

When I took this off the menu at my restaurant, there was such an outcry from customers that we had to put it back on after just 2 weeks. I'm not sure I can give it a better introduction than that! Make sure you buy undyed smoked haddock or trout.

Serves 4

2 tablespoons butter
1 onion, finely diced
1 leek, finely sliced
2 garlic cloves, crushed
1/2 cup dry white wine
1 1/4 cups fish stock
3/4 cup milk
7 oz potatoes, peeled and diced
1 1/3 lb undyed smoked haddock or trout, skin removed and cut into small chunks
16 fresh mussels, scrubbed and debearded
2/3 cup half-and-half
6 chives, finely sliced
sea salt and freshly ground black pepper

Set a saucepan over medium heat and melt the butter. Stir in the onion, leek, and garlic. Reduce the heat, cover, and leave to sweat for 5 minutes.

Remove the pan from the heat and add the wine. Return the pan to the heat and cook for another 3-4 minutes. Pour in the stock, milk, and potatoes and bring to a boil. Reduce the heat and simmer for 10 minutes.

Stir in the trout and mussels and continue to cook for 5 minutes. Add the cream, chives, and season to taste with salt and pepper. Cook for another 5 minutes.

PARMESAN AND ROSEMARY POLENTA FRIES

A favorite of mine after a trip to Emilio Romania in Italy. A great snack for movie watching, a great side dish with roasted chicken, and great for party food.

Serves 8

2$\frac{1}{4}$ cups water
2$\frac{1}{4}$ lb polenta
2 cups Parmesan cheese, grated
vegetable oil, for deep-frying
a few sprigs of rosemary
sea salt and freshly ground black pepper

Line a baking sheet with parchment paper.

Bring the water to a boil in a large saucepan, add the polenta, and stir over medium-high heat for about 20 minutes.

Reduce the heat, stir in the Parmesan, season to taste with salt and pepper, and continue to stir for another 5 minutes.

Spread the polenta in the baking sheet to an even depth of about $\frac{1}{2}$ in. Allow to cool and then cut the polenta into french fry-like shapes.

Deep-fry the polenta and toss them in sea salt and finely chopped rosemary to serve.

SPICY CHICKEN WINGS

I love serving these spicy and sweet wings with a cooling blue cheese dip. Just whisk together $3\frac{1}{2}$ oz blue cheese, $\frac{1}{2}$ cup sour cream and the juice of $\frac{1}{2}$ lemon.

Makes 36

36 chicken wings
6 garlic cloves, crushed
1 teaspoon freshly grated ginger
2 teaspoons sesame oil
$\frac{1}{2}$ cup light soy sauce
2 tablespoons rice wine vinegar
2 tablespoons vegetable oil
2 tablespoons Tabasco sauce
1 tablespoon brown sugar
sea salt and freshly ground black pepper

To serve

6 chives, snipped
1 cup sour cream

Preheat the oven to 350°F. Line a baking sheet with aluminum foil.

Season the wings with salt and pepper, put them on the baking sheet, and bake in the oven for 45 minutes.

Make a vinaigrette by whisking together the remaining ingredients. Pour the vinaigrette over the wings while they are hot and toss them around so that the wings soak up all the dressing.

Scatter the chives over the wings and serve with sour cream.

MINI SPICY MEATBALLS

To make these more moist add 3½ oz ricotta cheese.
Delicious served with my Tomato, Basil, and Olive Sauce
on page 195.

Makes 40

6½ lb ground beef
6 tablespoons chopped
fresh cilantro
4 red chiles, finely
chopped
6 garlic cloves, crushed
2 onions, finely chopped
3 eggs, lightly beaten
flour, for dusting
olive oil, for frying
sea salt and freshly
ground black pepper

Preheat the oven to 350°F.

In a large bowl mix together the beef,
cilantro, chiles, garlic, onions, and eggs.
Season to taste with salt and pepper.

Roll a teaspoon of the beef mixture into a
ball, dust it in flour, and put to one side.
Repeat with the rest of the mixture.

Set a frying pan over medium heat and add some
olive oil. Gently sauté the meatballs and then
cook them in the oven for 15 minutes.

Serve with Roasted Tomato, Basil, and Olive
Sauce (see page 195) to dip the meatballs in.

CHICKEN, BROCCOLI, AND PARMESAN CASSEROLE

A crispy topping, creamy base, with crunchy broccoli bites—delicious. Serve with a big green salad.

Serves 4

2 tablespoons olive oil

2 skinless chicken fillets, diced

1 onion, finely chopped

2 garlic cloves, crushed

2 tablespoons butter

¼ cup flour

¾ cup milk

1 cup Parmesan cheese, grated

10 basil leaves, torn

10 cups broccoli, quartered and blanched

1 cup breadcrumbs

½ cup pine nuts, chopped

sea salt and freshly ground black pepper

Preheat the oven to 350°F.

Set a saucepan over medium heat and add the oil. Stir in the chicken, season with salt and pepper, and cook for 3 minutes, searing on all sides. Stir in the onion and garlic and cook for another 2 minutes.

Set a separate saucepan over low heat to make the sauce. Melt the butter, stir in the flour, and continue to stir until the flour is cooked and you get a paste (roux). Whisk in the milk, a little at a time, until you have a thick, creamy béchamel sauce. Whisk in the Parmesan and basil and season with salt and pepper.

Put the seared chicken and onions into a roasting pan or large ovenproof dish and arrange the broccoli around the chicken. Pour the Parmesan and basil sauce over the chicken. Sprinkle the breadcrumbs and pine nuts on top and cook in the oven for 20 minutes.

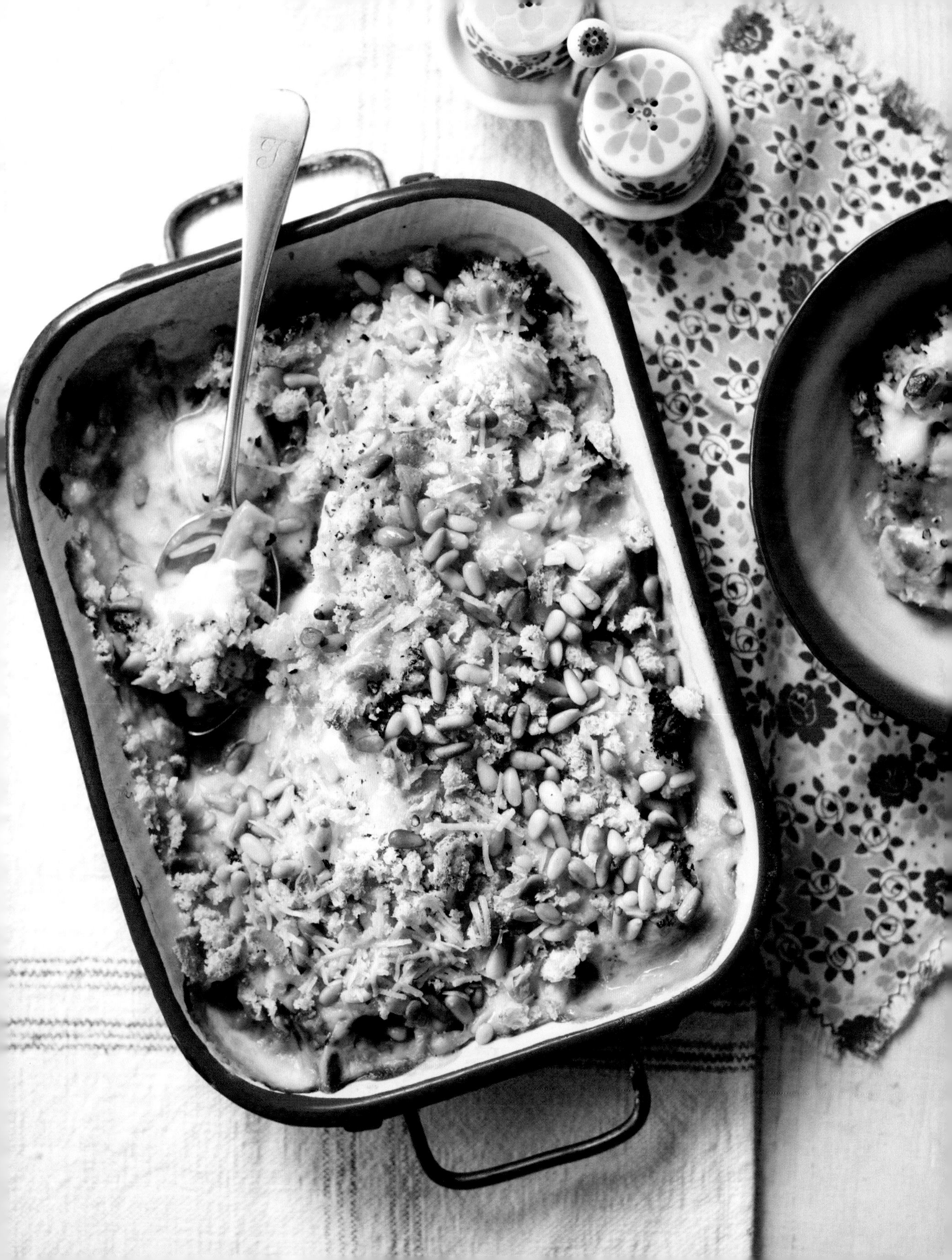

CHICKEN, TARRAGON, AND MUSHROOM PIE

This is comfort food at its best. I made mini versions of this recipe for the designer Anya Hindmarch's launch in Ireland, they were delicious. They freeze perfectly too.

Serves 4

2 tablespoons butter
4 skinless chicken cutlets, diced
1 leek, finely sliced
3¼ cups button mushrooms, quartered
1 tablespoon flour
1 cup milk
½ cup half-and-half
2 tablespoons chopped tarragon leaves
1-lb pack of puff pastry (use butter puff or brush ordinary puff with a little butter)
1 egg, beaten

Preheat the oven to 400°F.

Set a large pan over medium heat and melt the butter. Add the chicken, season with salt and pepper, and cook for 5 minutes. Stir in the leek and cook for another minute.

Add the mushrooms to the pan and cook for 3 minutes. Sprinkle over the flour, stir, and cook for another minute, then pour in the milk and half-and-half and allow to cook until the sauce has thickened. Stir in the chopped tarragon.

Roll out the pastry and cut it into four pieces big enough to cover four small pie dishes. Spoon the chicken mixture into the dishes and brush the rims with beaten egg.

Lift the pastry on to the pies, trimming off any excess. Press down and crimp the edges with a fork. Cut a couple of slits in the pastry to let the steam out and brush all over with the rest of the egg. Bake in the oven for 15-20 minutes or until the pastry is crisp and golden brown.

LEMON AND ROSEMARY ROAST CHICKEN

I do a roast chicken about once a month, investing in
good-quality, organic chicken because it tastes
far better.

Serves 4

7 tablespoons butter
2 lemons
4 sprigs of rosemary,
finely chopped
5 garlic cloves, crushed
1 whole chicken
2 lb potatoes, peeled
and quartered
16 shallots, left whole
sea salt and freshly
ground black pepper
olive oil

Preheat the oven to 350°F.

In a bowl mix together the butter, lemon juice and
zest, the finely chopped rosemary leaves and garlic,
and season with salt and pepper. Spread half the
flavored butter over the chicken.

Chop up the lemon skins and place them in the cavity
of the chicken along with the rosemary stalks left
once you have removed the leaves.

Set a roasting pan over low heat and add the remaining
flavored butter. Melt the butter, increase the heat,
and toss the potatoes and shallots until well coated.
Arrange the vegetables around the sides of the
roasting pan and put the chicken in the center.

Roast in the oven for $1^{1}/_{2}$ hours. Every 20 minutes
spoon the juices in the roasting pan over the chicken
to enhance the flavor.

CHILI

This is always better the next day as the flavors develop overnight. This chili, some sour cream, guacamole, and rice in front of an open fire and a great movie is November heaven to me.

Serves 4

1 tablespoon olive oil

1 onion, finely chopped

3 garlic cloves, crushed

1 red bell pepper, cored, seeded, and finely chopped

1 tablespoon freshly grated ginger

1 teaspoon hot chili powder

1 teaspoon paprika

1 teaspoon ground cinnamon

1 teaspoon ground cumin

1 lb ground beef

14-oz can chopped tomatoes

1 teaspoon dried oregano

1 teaspoon brown sugar

2 tablespoons tomato paste

1¼ cups hot stock (preferably beef stock)

14-oz can red kidney beans, rinsed and drained

sea salt and freshly ground black pepper

Place a large saucepan or baking dish over medium heat and add the oil. Stir in the onion, garlic, red bell pepper, ginger, chili powder, paprika, cinnamon, and cumin, cover and leave to simmer for 2-3 minutes.

In a separate pan brown the ground beef, season with salt and pepper, and add to the onion mixture.

Stir in the tomatoes, dried oregano, sugar, tomato paste, and stock. Bring to a boil, reduce the heat, and allow to simmer for 20 minutes. Lastly stir in the kidney beans and cook for another 5 minutes.

Burrito—To make a burrito, spoon some chili into a tortilla with shredded lettuce and some Lime and Tomato Guacamole (see page 140) and wrap it up.

PAPPARDELLE WITH BEEF RAGU

The secret to a great ragu is the longer you leave it to simmer over low heat, the better it tastes. If it gets too dry just stir in some water. If you can't get pappardelle then use spaghetti. This freezes well, so double up and save for a rainy, hungry evening.

Serves 4

2-3 tablespoons olive oil

2 tablespoons butter

1 onion, finely diced

1 carrot, finely diced

½ celery stalk, finely diced

4 garlic cloves, crushed

2¼ lb ground beef

1⅔ cups red wine

21-oz can chopped tomatoes

2 tablespoons tomato paste

2 teaspoons dried oregano

1 teaspoon freshly grated nutmeg

1⅓ cups fresh pappardelle

1 cup Parmesan cheese, grated

sea salt and freshly ground black pepper

Set a baking dish over medium heat and add the oil and butter. Add the onion, carrot, celery, and garlic, stir and cook for 5 minutes or until softened.

Stir in the beef and season with salt and pepper. Cook, stirring occasionally, until the beef has turned a light brown color. Pour in the wine and leave to simmer for about 20 minutes.

Stir in the tomatoes, tomato paste, dried oregano, and nutmeg, season with salt and pepper and mix well. Reduce the heat and leave to simmer for an hour or more if you can. The longer you allow it to simmer the more tender and flavorsome the ragu becomes. Add a little beef stock if it becomes too thick.

Put a large saucepan of salted water over high heat and bring to a boil. Add in the pappardelle and continue to stir for 2 minutes. Cook until al dente and drain, reserving 2 tablespoons of cooking water. Return the pasta to the saucepan (off the heat) and stir in the cooking water followed by the ragu.

Serve with grated Parmesan sprinkled over the dish.

NAAN BREAD

I have a wonderful Indian chef working for me called Jamille. He taught me how to make Naan bread and now we serve them with our house Indian Chicken Curry. You can add a whole variety of toppings, see below.

Makes 5

For the dough

2 cups all-purpose flour
2 teaspoons sugar
$\frac{1}{2}$ teaspoon salt
$\frac{1}{2}$ teaspoon baking powder
about $\frac{1}{2}$ cup milk
2 tablespoons vegetable oil, plus extra for greasing

For the topping

poppy seeds or sesame seeds, or chopped garlic and fresh cilantro
melted butter

Make the dough. Sift the flour, sugar, salt, and baking powder into a bowl. In another bowl mix together the milk and oil.

Make a well in the center of the flour mixture and pour in the liquid. Slowly mix the dough, working from the center and incorporating the flour from the edges of the well, to make a smooth, soft dough. Knead well for 8-10 minutes, adding a little flour if the dough is too sticky.

Place the dough into an oiled bowl, cover with a damp kitchen towel and leave in a warm place for 10-15 minutes. Form the dough into five balls.

Preheat the broiler to medium and put a heavy baking sheet on the upper shelf of the broiler to heat.

Roll the dough balls out quite thinly, ideally in a teardrop shape. Sprinkle over your chosen topping and press into the surface of the dough. Place the naan bread on the hot baking sheet and broil for 1-2 minutes or until lightly browned. Brush with butter and serve hot.

INDIAN CURRY

I absolutely love this recipe. You could try replacing the chicken with lamb if you wish. Serve with raita.

Serves 4

3-in piece of fresh ginger, peeled and finely chopped

6 garlic cloves, chopped

1 onion, finely chopped

1 tablespoon ground coriander

1 tablespoon ground cumin

$1/2$ teaspoon ground turmeric

1 teaspoon cayenne pepper

$3/4$ cup water

3 tablespoons vegetable oil

4 skinless chicken cutlets, diced

$3/4$ cup coconut milk

$3^1/2$oz can chopped tomatoes

$2^1/4$ cups butternut squash, diced

24 green beans

2 tablespoons fresh cilantro, chopped

sea salt and freshly ground black pepper

Put the ginger, garlic, onion, and spices into a food processor with $1/3$ cup water and blend to a fine paste. You may have to push the mixture down with a spatula from time to time. Set aside.

Heat the oil in a large, wide, preferably nonstick pan, over high heat. Stir in the chicken, season with salt and pepper, and cook for 3-4 minutes.

Add the spicy paste to the pan with the remaining water, coconut milk, and tomatoes. Bring to a boil, stir in the butternut squash, cover, reduce the heat to low, and cook for 20 minutes.

Stir in the green beans and cook for another 5 minutes. Remove the pan from the heat and stir in the fresh cilantro. Check the seasoning and serve with naan bread and raita.

RAITA

Serves 4

$1/2$ cucumber

$1/2$ red onion, finely chopped

$2^1/4$ cups Greek yogurt

2 tablespoons chopped mint leaves

2 tablespoons chopped fresh cilantro leaves

sea salt and freshly ground black pepper

Coarsely grate the cucumber into a bowl and squeeze it with your hands to remove as much juice as possible.

In a bowl mix together the cucumber, onion, yogurt, mint, and cilantro. Season with salt and pepper. Cover with plastic wrap and chill until you are ready to serve.

APPLE, CINNAMON, AND RAISIN BREAD AND BUTTER PUDDING

I'm a huge fan of bread and butter pudding. You can omit the apple if you wish, and add melted chocolate. Or sometimes, if I have leftover brioche I'll use it for a super decadent bread and butter pudding.

Serves 5

1²/₃ cups milk

1²/₃ cups half-and-half

¹/₂ cup superfine sugar

6 eggs

1 teaspoon vanilla extract

1 tablespoon ground cinnamon

16 slices of white bread, cut into triangles

1 cup cooking apples, quartered, cored and sliced

³/₄ cup golden raisins

Preheat the oven to 325°F.

Set a saucepan over medium heat, add the milk, half-and-half, and sugar and mix well together. Cook until the sugar has dissolved, then set aside to cool.

Whisk the eggs in a large bowl and stir in the vanilla extract and cinnamon. Whisk in the milk mixture.

Overlap the bread pieces and apple slices in an ovenproof dish and pour over the egg mixture. Use your hands to push the bread gently into the egg mixture so that it is completed immersed. Scatter the raisins over the top of the pudding. Bake in the oven for 45 minutes.

HOMEMADE CHRISTMAS WREATH

I've been a huge fan of Ruth Monahan's creativity for a long time. Imagine a modern day Audrey Hepburn in the most glorious flower shop and you have a picture of Ruth. Since establishing Appassionata Flowers (www.appassionata.ie) in 2004 with her husband Ultan, Ruth has brought a fresh and inspirational approach to flowers in Dublin. She started in her kitchen but has grown Appassionata into one of the market leaders in the field of quality floristry design. I'm so happy that she is part of my book, and here is her guide to making a beautiful Christmas wreath.

Preparation

Making the Christmas wreath is one of the nicest things to do in preparation for the festive season. The best time to start planning your wreath is in late November, so you will be ready to display it from about 2 weeks before the big day. It looks amazing to see all the doorways dressed with wreaths individually created to suit the person living there.

Before starting your wreath you need to consider several things. Your front door will define your wreath's look and feel. The color and size of your door will act as a background for your festive display. Also, consider what you will hang the wreath on so that it is secure and will defy rain, wind, and snow, not to mention children's curious hands.

Decide your preferred color scheme. Do you want to go red and traditional, dusky blue and vintage, or shun the traditional festive colors and make it pink? It's always good to have saved some autumnal hydrangea in your preferred color scheme, and we always have old heads hanging in bunches around the studio and shop ready to dress our Christmas wreaths.

Your tools are the secret to a beautiful and successful wreath. You will need a glue gun, a wire frame base or a noble pine base, a reel of wire, lots of noble pine, and a gorgeous ribbon to adorn the doorway. How you dress your wreath comes down to you prefered textures and scents. You might like to try eucalyptus and lavender (for a calming scent as you reach home), skimmia (can be bought as plant or cut), thistle (in blue or white), berries (such as hypericum, viburnum and ilex), or dried hydrangea (it looks fresh as the day it was cut and beats silk versions hands down). Noble pine can be bought in bunches from a florist or garden center, and other elements you could grab from the nursery or a garden center include rosemary, moss or lichen, cones, cinnamon, and mini apples.

Making a Wreath

I usually lay old newspapers out on my kitchen table, place all of the various elements in groups ready for action and have the glue gun heating up.

First cut the noble pine for the base of your wreath. Start the reel wire by winding it onto the frame. Gradually place the pine in layers

The best way to work is to go layer by layer each time using the glue gun to secure the element, e.g. eucalyptus, followed by skimmia, berries, and thistle. Make sure each sits securely in the pine base. Add lavender, rosemary, and extra berries to fill in any gaps. The wreath should look balanced and similar from all angles.

If using cinnamon and cones, wire them first. We usually cut a long cinnamon stick into three and fasten with a knot of ribbon. Reel wire wrapped around the stack of three with a long piece left to act as a stalk works well for placing into the wreath. Leave a gap where you would like to place the ribbon, wrap reel wire around the wreath and leave a long double strand trailing. Tie ribbon in a gorgeous four loop bow with trailing elements. Give your wreath a good spray of water before hanging so that it glistens,

along the circular frame. Continue binding the wire around and around the pine and frame until you have created a substantial base. You want the wreath to look bushy and full.

Now cut more pine in shorter pieces and continue the binding process. Keep turning the wreath after each insertion as this will help to create a nice full look. Trim any unruly pieces. Keep the wreath diameter to approximately 16in as this is the best dimension for a regular front door.

Separate the hydrangea heads into smaller pieces (unless you want the hydrangea to be completely dominant). Using the glue gun, add glue to the base of the stalk and insert at right angles into the pine. Work clockwise and keep turning the wreath to ensure evenness of placement.

All other elements should be cut short at an angle for easier insertion.

attach to the door securely with the wire, and be the envy of all your neighbors!

TIP Keep it sprayed with water every few days to keep it looking like the day it was made, otherwise the leaves will go curly and the berries all crinkly.

Winter Berry Sherry Trifle

DECEMBER

CHRISTMAS TRADITIONS

I love the way Christmas both passes on traditions and creates new ones.
The first Christmas I had in my own home in Monkstown, Dublin, changed the
whole way I thought about Christmas. It unleashed my inner Christmas
fairy. I decorated the tree with old hand-me-down decorations and tied
little birds, cherries, and figs to the branches. I tied cinnamon sticks
and dried orange skin into little bundles and threw them on the open fire
to give the house a wonderful spicy smell. After Mass on Christmas day it
was home for a hearty brunch. To work up an appetite for Christmas lunch,
which was served at five o'clock, we had a huge walk in the afternoon.
Making the centerpieces and an afternoon walk have become set in stone
household traditions.

A Christmas tradition I have established for myself is a shopping spree
in London a month or so before Christmas. I always visit Fortnum and
Mason on Piccadilly—the smell as soon as you walk in is the essence of
Christmas bottled. It's not just the wonderful foods I love, but the
beautiful tins and packaging too. I will always drop into the luxury
stationers, Smythson, for gifts. They do really funky colored notebooks
with little messages embossed on the front, like the "make it happen"
notebook. One unapologetically indulgent visit I make is to the Fumoir,
the art deco bar in Claridge's. I'd go just to look at the beautiful
cocktail glasses, never mind the intoxicating drinks! And finally,
something I have done since my twenties, I go to the opera at Covent
Garden and have a meal at the fish
restaurant, J.Sheekey.
I end my visit with a walk to
Trafalgar Square to see the
Christmas tree that Norway
traditionally sends Britain
every year.

POMEGRANATE CHAMPAGNE

This is a fun cocktail, the color is just so
Christmassy. A good prosecco like Valdo would work
perfectly here. Buy a couple of fresh pomegranates and
pop a few of the seeds into the glasses.

Makes 8

crushed ice
2¼ cups pomegranate
juice
½ cup ginger ale
⅓ cup brandy
1 bottle Champagne or
sparkling wine

Fill a large jug two-thirds of the way with
crushed ice. Add the rest of the ingredients
and mix well.

BAKED VACHERIN

Gooey, easy, and yummy. You can use other semisoft
cheeses too, such as Gubbeen or Durrus Irish Farmhouse.
Add a little bit of crushed garlic or finely chopped
fresh thyme.

Serves 4

1 lb box vacherin cheese
¼ cup dry white wine

Preheat the oven to 350°F. Wrap the base of the box
containing the cheese in aluminum foil.

Cut a cross on the top of the cheese and pour over
the wine. Put it on a baking sheet and cook in the
oven for 15-20 minutes, depending on how ripe the
cheese is.

Serve the cheese in the box, and let your guests scoop
out the gooey cheese with warm crusty bread.

280

PARMESAN CHEESE STRAWS

These are such fun to make. You can use any hard cheese that you wish and dip them in sesame seeds if you fancy the idea. Perfect for serving on their own or with dips.

Makes 26

1 egg

1 tablespoon water

1 lb sheet of ready-rolled puff pastry

1/2 cup Parmesan cheese, grated

1 teaspoon dried oregano leaves (optional)

Preheat the oven to 350°F. Grease a baking sheet.

In a small bowl whisk together the egg and water and set aside.

Unfold the pastry on a lightly floured surface and roll it out to a 14 × 10-in rectangle. Cut it in half lengthwise and brush both halves with the egg and water mixture.

Sprinkle the cheese and oregano, if using, over one rectangle and place the other rectangle on top, egg side down. Roll gently with a rolling pin to seal. Cut the pastry crosswise into 26 strips, each about 1/2-in wide.

Twist the strips and place them 2 in apart on the baking sheet, pressing down the ends. Brush with the egg and water mixture and bake in the oven for 10 minutes or until golden.

SESAME AND FENNEL MINI SAUSAGE ROLLS

These freeze extremely well and are delicious served with piccalilli or my House Chutney (see page 212).

Makes 20

¾ lb sausage meat or sausages

2 tablespoons chopped flat-leaf parsley

13 oz sheet of ready-rolled puff pastry

1 beaten egg, to glaze

1 tablespoon fennel seeds

1 tablespoon sesame seeds

sea salt and freshly ground black pepper

Preheat the oven to 350°F.

Put the sausage meat and flat-leaf parsley in a mixing bowl, season with salt and pepper, and stir well. Set aside.

Unroll the pastry onto a lightly floured board and cut it in half lengthwise to give two rectangles, each about 10 in long.

Halve the sausage mixture and roll each half into a cylinder, about 10 in long. Spread each roll along the length of each pastry strip, leaving a ½ in edge. Tightly roll the pastry around the sausage meat and brush the ends with the beaten egg to secure. Use a sharp knife to cut each roll into 10 pieces, each about 1 in long, and place them on a baking sheet.

Brush more egg over the pastry and sprinkle the fennel and sesame seeds on top of the sausage rolls. Cook in the oven for 25-35 minutes until the pastry is puffed and crisp and the meat has cooked through.

CRAB AND AVOCADO TOASTS

This is a staple of mine to serve at Christmas parties.
They are the perfect bite, and look so pretty. You can
also use this recipe as a salad for a starter or lunch.
Just bed the plates with lots of fresh arugula, then
sprinkle the crab mix over, and instead of mashing the
avocado, slice it and arrange on top of the crab mix.
Serve the toasted baguettes on the side.

Serves 6

1 French baguette

2 tablespoons extra
virgin olive oil

1 1/2 cups crab meat,
cooked

2 teaspoons lime juice

1 tablespoon chopped
mint

2 Hass avocados

a pinch of cayenne
pepper

sea salt and freshly
ground black pepper

Preheat the oven to 350°F.

Thinly slice the baguette and lightly brush the slices
with oil. Transfer to a baking sheet and cook in the
oven for 3-4 minutes or until lightly golden.

In a bowl mix together the crab meat and mint and
season with salt and pepper. In a separate, smaller
bowl mash the avocado flesh with lime juice, a pinch
each of salt and cayenne pepper.

Spread the mashed avocado over the sliced bread, top
with the crab mixture and serve.

ORANGE AND CINNAMON MINCE PIE ROULADES

I came up with this recipe at the cooking school when I was looking for stress-free foods I could serve over Christmas. They are so delicious, best served warm and with heavy cream.

Makes 12

½ cup superfine sugar
1 sheet of ready-rolled puff pastry
1 egg yolk
1 tablespoon milk
3 cups Christmas Mincemeat (see page 249)
1 tablespoon flaked almonds
zest of 1 orange
1 teaspoon ground cinnamon
confectioners' sugar, for dusting

Preheat the oven to 400°F.

Scatter the sugar over the work surface, unroll the pastry, and roll it out to 14 x 9 in.

Whisk the egg yolk with the milk. Spread the mincemeat evenly over the pastry, leaving a 1in border along the longer edges. Fold one of the longer edges over the mincemeat, then roll the pastry tightly into a sausage shape while gently pressing the pastry into the mincemeat. When you get to the other edge, brush it with milk and egg and press it down to seal in the mincemeat. Press both ends in gently to plump up the roll and chill for at least 30 minutes to firm it. (The mincemeat roll may now be frozen whole or as portioned slices, see below, and kept for up to a month.)

Cut the roll into 12 rounds, each about 1in thick. Lay them evenly spaced on a large baking sheet and flatten them with your hand so they resemble squashed scones. Scatter over the flaked almonds and orange zest, sprinkle the ground cinnamon on top, and bake for 20-30 minutes until golden brown and the mincemeat sizzles. Leave to cool for 5 minutes; keep them separate so they don't stick together.

Sift confectioners' sugar over the slices before serving.

CHRISTMAS LIST

Make your Christmas cake
Order your meat
Make a homemade wreath
Buy stocking fillers
Write and send your
Christmas cards
Bake and wrap edible
gifts for your friends
and family
Decorate the tree!

I love the way Christmas both passes on traditons and creates new ones.

SMOKED SALMON TERRINE WITH DILL AND LEMON CREAM

This is the perfect starter for when you have guests coming. You can make it the day before and leave it in the fridge until it is time to serve.

Serves 8

1 lb cream cheese, softened

$^1/_3$ cup heavy cream

zest of 1 lemon

2 tablespoons lemon juice

3 tablespoons fresh dill, finely chopped

2 tablespoons capers, drained

$1^1/_3$ lb sliced smoked salmon, sliced

sea salt and freshly ground black pepper

To serve

1 bunch watercress, trimmed

brown bread

Make the dill and lemon cream. Place the cream cheese, cream, lemon zest, lemon juice, dill, and capers in a food processor, season with salt and pepper, and blend to combine.

Grease a 3 x 4 x 8 in loaf pan. Line the base and sides of the pan with plastic wrap, allowing a 2 in overhang on the long sides.

Trim any brown edges from the salmon. Cover the base of the pan with 1 layer of smoked salmon. Using a spatula, spread $^1/_3$ of the cream cheese mixture over the salmon. Add another salmon layer on top, followed by another cream cheese layer. Repeat until the cream cheese mixture is used, finishing with a salmon layer. Fold the plastic wrap over the top, press down gently, and refrigerate overnight.

Before serving, turn the terrine out. Remove the plastic wrap, and trim the ends. Serve with watercress and some homemade brown bread.

CELERY ROOT AND HAZELNUT SOUP

Celery root and hazelnut are such a great combination. This is a very creamy soup; the hazelnuts add a deep nutty flavor and crunch. Try adding celery root to creamy mashed potato the next time you cook it.

Serves 6

2 tablespoons butter

$^2/_3$ cup onions, chopped

$^1/_4$ lb potatoes, peeled and chopped

1 lb celery root, peeled and chopped

1 quart hot chicken stock

$^3/_4$ cup half-and-half

2 tablespoons chopped hazelnuts

1 tablespoon finely chopped flat-leaf parsley

sea salt and freshly ground black pepper

Set a saucepan over medium and melt the butter. Stir in the onions, potatoes, and celery root, cover and leave to sweat for 10 minutes, checking and stirring every few minutes. Remove the lid and cook for another 5 minutes, stirring every minute, to help build up the flavor.

Pour the stock over the vegetables and continue to cook until all the vegetable are cooked through.

Add the cream, stir, and season to taste with salt and pepper. Blend with an immersion blender or food processor until smooth and creamy.

Toast the chopped hazelnuts in a hot oven or in a dry frying pan. Sprinkle a few nuts over each serving of soup together with some parsley.

ORANGE, CINNAMON, AND STAR ANISE TURKEY GLAZE

Not only is this glaze perfect for glazing turkey or ham, it also works as a beautiful glaze for non-iced Christmas cakes!

juice of 4 oranges
1 cup granulated sugar
1 cinnamon stick
1 star anise

Pour the juice of 4 oranges, sugar, cinnamon, and star anise into a saucepan set over high heat. Stir every 30 seconds until the sugar has dissolved into the juice.

Bring the liquid to a boil, reduce the heat, and leave to simmer for 15 minutes.

Remove the pan from the heat and allow to cool. The syrup will thicken as it cools.

CHRISTMAS TURKEY TIPS

Whether you're cooking a turkey for Christmas or Thanksgiving, if you are using a frozen turkey it's best to thaw the bird in the fridge. A turkey will need about 24 hours to thaw for every 4-5 lb. If your turkey is fresh it is best to store it in the fridge if at all possible.

Take the turkey out of the fridge 45 minutes before roasting to allow the meat to relax and come to room temperature, which will make the meat more tender.

To prepare the turkey for cooking remove the giblets from inside the bird's cavity because these cannot be cooked with the turkey. Keep them for when you are making turkey stock or gravy. Wash the cavity and make sure it is completely dry with paper towels.

Stuffing that is cooked inside a turkey is definitely tastier than stuffing cooked separately, but you must make sure that the stuffing is cool and fill only half the cavity. Tie the legs together with twine. If you decided to cook the stuffing separately use the juices from the cooked turkey to keep the stuffing moist.

If possible place a wire rack in the roasting pan for the turkey to sit on. This will allow the juices and fat to drain off, and you can use them to baste the turkey while it is cooking to create a tastier meat.

Tuck potatoes around the turkey so they soak up the delicious flavors.

Use a good-quality cranberry sauce or apple jelly as a glaze for the turkey. Use a pastry brush to paint the bird with the sauce or jelly and baste every 30 minutes.

Check to see if the turkey is cooked by inserting a skewer into the thickest part of the thigh; the juices should run clear.

When you have taken the turkey out of the oven leave it to rest for 30 minutes with a loose tent of aluminum foil over the bird to keep it warm. This will allow the juices to redistribute themselves, giving tastier meat.

TURKEY COOKING TIMES

You should always allow 15 minutes per pound, plus an additional 15 minutes.

7.5-11 lb	12-14 lb	14-15.5 lb	17.5-20 lb	20-24 lb
3 hours 20 minutes - 4 hours 40 minutes	4 hours 40 minutes - 5 hours 20 minutes	5 hours 20 minutes - 6 hours 40 minutes	6 hours 40 minutes - 7 hours 20 minutes	7 hours 20 minutes - 8 hours 40 minutes
3 hours - 4 hours 20 minutes	4 hours 20 mins - 5 hours	5 hours - 6 hours 20 minutes	6 hours 20 minutes - 7 hours	7 hours - 8 hours 20 minutes

THE PERFECT ROASTED POTATOES

I think Maris Pipers or King Edwards make the best roasted potatoes, as they provide a fluffy inside to your crispy skin. And yes, goose fat is essential. Go on it's Christmas!

Serves 8

4 lb potatoes, peeled
3 tablespoons goose fat
3 tablespoons chopped thyme leaves
sea salt and freshly ground black pepper

Preheat the oven to 400°F.

Cut the potatoes in half or in quarters if they are very big: they should all be similar in size. Put them into a saucepan of cold salted water, bring to a boil and cook for 8 minutes. Drain.

Put the goose fat in a roasting pan over a hot stove. When it is hot, stir in the thyme leaves. Add the potatoes and season with salt and pepper. Toss in the fat and cook in the oven for 30 minutes.

MUSTARD GLAZED CARROTS, SHALLOTS, AND PARSNIPS

You can add fennel, rutabaga, and celery root to the mix if you wish. Make the glaze the day before and refrigerate, one less thing to do on Christmas day!

Serves 6

4 tablespoons butter
1 tablespoon cider vinegar
3 tablespoons grainy mustard
3 tablespoons light brown sugar
12 shallots, root ends trimmed
1 lb carrots, cut into 2 in pieces
1 lb parsnips, cut into 2 in pieces
sea salt and freshly ground pepper

Preheat the oven to 400°F

Melt the butter and pour it into a bowl. Add the vinegar, mustard, and sugar and whisk together.

Put the vegetables in a roasting pan, pour over the mustard glaze, and mix well. Season with salt and pepper and cook in the oven for 35-40 minutes or until tender.

SPICED RED CABBAGE

The color of this recipe is fantastic, it adds so much
flavor to a Christmas table. It will last for up to
4 days in the fridge.

Serves 6

5 tablespoons butter

9 cups red cabbage, shredded

1/2 onion, thinly sliced

1 teaspoon ground cinnamon

1 teaspoon ground nutmeg

6 cloves

1/3 cup red wine vinegar

1/2 cup brown sugar

about 3 cups cooking apples, peeled, cored, and sliced

sea salt and freshly ground black pepper

Set a large, heavy-bottomed saucepan or baking dish over medium heat and add the butter. Add the cabbage and onion, stir well and cook for a few minutes to soften.

Season with salt and pepper and stir in the spices. Add the vinegar and sugar and allow to cook for another 5 minutes.

Put the apples on top, cover, and leave for 10 minutes. Remove the lid, stir, and leave to cook for another 10-15 minutes.

SPICED CRANBERRY SAUCE

You can substitute the fresh cranberries for apricots
or plums and this sauce will be equally delicious.

Serves 6

1 cup granulated sugar
½ cup water
14 oz cranberries
3-in piece of fresh
ginger
10 whole cloves
1 whole red chile
cinnamon stick

Put the sugar, water, and cranberries in a saucepan.

Use the tip of a small teaspoon to peel the fresh
ginger, and stud the ginger with the cloves. Add the
ginger to the saucepan along with the chile and the
cinnamon stick.

Set the saucepan over high heat and bring to a boil,
stirring every 30 seconds to make sure that the sugar
dissolves. When the cranberries have popped, reduce
the heat to a simmer and allow to cook for another
10 minutes.

The cranberry sauce is best served at room
temperature. Cranberry sauce will thicken when it is
chilled, so if you make it a few days in advance and
add a little water to the saucepan before adding the
sauce and warm it gently.

VARIATIONS

For spiced orange and cranberry sauce

Replace the ginger
with freshly squeezed
orange juice.

For spiced plum sauce

Replace the
cranberries
with quartered
and stoned
fresh plums.

SAGE, PANCETTA, AND DATE STUFFING

This could be looked upon as my Italian influence on my otherwise traditional Irish Christmas lunch. The sweetness from the dates, smokiness from the pancetta, and earthiness from the sage make an incredible stuffing.

Serves 8

7 oz pancetta, chopped

1 large onion, finely diced

3 tablespoons chopped sage

²/₃ cup dates, finely chopped

1¹/₂ lb good-quality pork sausages, skins removed

¹/₃ cup fresh white breadcrumbs

2 tablespoons chopped parsley

1 teaspoon freshly grated nutmeg

sea salt and freshly ground black pepper

Set a frying pan over medium heat and cook the pancetta for about 4 minutes or until golden. Stir in the onion and cook for another 5 minutes. Transfer to a bowl.

Stir in the sage, dates, sausage meat, breadcrumbs, parsley, and nutmeg. Season with salt and pepper and mix well.

Makes 24

1 bottle of good red
wine
$1/2$ cup raw unrefined sugar
rind of 1 lemon
rind of 1 orange
stick of cinnamon
3 cloves
splash of brandy

MULLED WINE

Probably the easiest thing for you to make over Christmas—it's brimming with Christmas spices. Add some sloe gin if you have it. Serve with a slice of orange.

Set a large, heavy-bottomed saucepan over low heat. Add all the ingredients to the pan and stir until all the sugar has dissolved and the wine is hot, but drinkable.

WINTER BERRY SHERRY TRIFLE

I use pound cake in my trifle as it absorbs all the delicious flavors of the crème cassis and berries and also adds its own flavor. Make sure you buy good quality custard, no canned custard need enter!

Serves 8

1 lb frozen mixed berries
1/3 cup superfine sugar
1/4 cup crème de cassis
7-oz pound cake, sliced
1 cup mascarpone cheese
1 tablespoon vanilla extract
2 cups custard
1 1/4 cups heavy cream, softly whipped

Put the berries and sugar in a saucepan over low heat and simmer for 2 minutes. Stir in the crème de cassis and set aside to cool.

Arrange a layer of pound cake slices at the bottom of a large trifle bowl and spoon two-thirds of the berry mix on top.

In a mixing bowl whisk together the mascarpone, vanilla extract, and custard until smooth; take care that it does not become too runny. Spoon the custard mixture on top of the cake and berries and top with the whipped cream.

Chill for a couple of hours in a fridge. Just before serving pour the remaining berries on top.

LEMON PASTRY MINCE PIES

You can use the zest of orange if you prefer. Chill your pastry cases in the fridge before you bake, they will be more buttery as a result.

Makes 16-24

melted butter, for greasing
1²/₃ cups all-purpose flour, sifted
zest of 1 lemon
1 tablespoon confectioners' sugar
7 tablespoons chilled unsalted butter, cubed
1 egg, beaten, plus extra for glazing
Christmas Mincemeat (see page 237)

Preheat the oven to 400°F. Lightly grease a shallow 24-hole cupcake cake pan or a 16-hole muffin pan.

Put the flour, lemon zest, confectioners' sugar and butter in a food processor and blend briefly. Add half the beaten egg and continue to blend. You might add a little more egg, but not too much as the mixture should be just moist enough to come together. If you are making the pastry by hand, rub the butter into the flour until it resembles coarse breadcrumbs, then, using your hands, add just enough egg to bring it together.

With your hands, flatten out the ball of dough until it is about 1in thick. Wrap it in plastic wrap or put it in a plastic bag and leave it in the fridge for at least 30 minutes or, if you are pushed for time, in the freezer for 10-15 minutes.

On a lightly floured work surface roll out the pastry to 1-in thick. Use a 2¹/₂-in (or an 3-in cutter if you are using a muffin pan) cutter to cut out 24 circles for the bases, and use a smaller plain or fluted cutter or star cutter to cut out 24 circles or stars for the lids. Re-roll the trimmings if necessary.

Line the holes of the cake pan with the larger pastry rounds. Fill each base with a teaspoon of mincemeat and top with one of the smaller rounds or stars. Brush the tops of the mince pies with beaten egg and cook in the oven for 15-20 minutes.

TURKEY CURRY

I don't know about you but I always cook too much
turkey. I was determined to create a curry that would
wow me nearly as much as the Christmas dinner. Serve
with Basmati Rice, my Raita on page 273, and my Naan
Bread on page 272.

Serves 6

3 tablespoons olive oil

1 large onion,
finely chopped

4 garlic cloves,
finely chopped

2-in piece of fresh
ginger, peeled
and grated

1 red chile, seeded and
finely chopped

8 green cardamom pods,
pods removed

1 teaspoon ground cumin

1 tablespoon ground
turmeric

1 teaspoon garam masala

1 teaspoon ground
coriander seeds

2 large potatoes,
peeled and diced

1 butternut squash,
peeled, seeded,
and diced

2½ cups chicken or
turkey stock

½ cup yogurt

⅓ cup heavy cream

1 tablespoon lemon juice

5 oz turkey, cooked
and chopped

1 tablespoon chopped
fresh cilantro leaves

sea salt and freshly
ground black pepper

Set a large baking dish over medium heat and pour in
the oil. Stir in the onion, garlic, ginger, chile,
cardamom seeds, cumin, turmeric, garam masala, and
ground coriander. Cover and sweat for 3-4 minutes
until the onions are soft; take care not to burn
the spices.

Stir in the potatoes and butternut squash and cook
until the potato begins to stick to the bottom of the
dish slightly.

Pour in the stock and bring to a boil. Season to taste
with salt and pepper. Reduce the heat and simmer for
10-15 minutes or until the potatoes and butternut
squash are tender.

Stir in the yogurt and cream, then add the lemon juice
and turkey. Simmer to heat through, sprinkle with
cilantro, and serve immediately.

CINNAMON AND BERRY GRANOLA BARS

Use any dried berries you wish. If you are not a fan of cinnamon, replace it with 1 teaspoon of vanilla extract.

Makes 12 bars

- 7 tablespoon butter, plus extra for greasing
- 7 cups steel-cut oats
- ¾ cup sunflower seeds
- ⅓ cup sesame seeds
- ½ cup chopped walnuts
- 3 tablespoons honey
- ¾ cup dark brown sugar
- 1 teaspoon ground cinnamon
- ¾ cup dried cranberries, cherries, or blueberries, or a mixture

Preheat the oven to 325°F. Butter and line the base of a 7 × 10-in pan.

Mix the oats, seeds, and nuts in a roasting pan and toast them in the oven for 5-10 minutes.

Meanwhile, put the butter, honey, and sugar in a saucepan and stir until the butter has melted. Add the oat mixture, cinnamon, and dried fruit and mix until the oats are well coated.

Put the mixture into the pan, press down lightly, and bake in the oven for 30 minutes. Leave to cool in the pan, then carefully remove and cut into 12 bars.

WHITE CHOCOLATE, HAZELNUT, AND CRANBERRY CHRISTMAS COOKIES

Wrapped in a pretty bag or box these cookies make a lovely edible Christmas gift. You can freeze or refrigerate the dough.

Makes 24 cookies

- 2½ sticks butter, softened
- ⅔ cup superfine sugar
- 2½ cups all-purpose flour
- 1 teaspoon baking powder
- 3 oz white chocolate, chopped
- ½ cup hazelnuts, chopped
- ½ cup dried cranberries, chopped

Preheat the oven to 350°F.

Put the butter and sugar in a large bowl and cream together with a wooden spoon until pale in color.

Sift the flour and baking powder into the bowl. Add the chocolate, hazelnuts, and cranberries and bring the mixture together to form a dough.

Divide the dough into three pieces and roll each piece into a sausage shape. Chill in the fridge for 1 hour.

Cut each roll into 8 slices and bake in the oven for 10-15 minutes.

INDEX

INDEX

INDEX

INDEX

DEDICATION

I dedicate my book to my 3 older siblings (yes I'm the baby!). My brother Jim for always making sure that I walked on the inside of the path and always being their for me through everything. My sister Mairead for being the backbone to our family, your strength is so inspiring and comforting to me, and Niamh for having a true heart of gold. I love you more than words can say and feel so blessed to have such a special closeness with you all. Thank you for all your encouragement and belief.
Family Forever, Clo xxxx

ACKNOWLEDGMENTS

When creating a cookbook, endless hours of creativity, passion, and commitment are given to the project by so many people. Firstly I would like to thank Kyle Cathie, an incredible woman who I look up to immensely. Kyle, you fabulous woman, masses of gratitude for letting me share my recipes, food, and above all for believing in me.

Kate Whitaker, photographer, what can I say? A beautiful lady in the truest sense of the meaning. She quietly does her magic while we all stand back in silenced awe. Your wonderful eye has brought my recipes to life. You have such an incredible talent and I hope to be lucky enough to work with you again and again. Lizzie Harris, the kitchen angel, how gorgeous it was to work with you. You are so calm and serene, not to mention a fantastic cook, you need to have your own book—you are too talented not to! Emily Kyd, thank you so much for your great cooking and for making those macaroons in the London summer heat! Penny Markham, prop stylist, thank you for foraging the most beautiful dishes, plates, and glasses for my food to fill! Emma Bastow, editor, thank you for your diligence and commitment to the book and for being so patient with me! Lucy Parissi, art direction and design, thank you for the wonderful design. Production team, Gemma John and Nic Jones, thank you!

For all on my home turf, my sister-in-law and best friend Erin McKenna, for your constant encouragement and keeping everything afloat in my life! Michael Andrews (aka Arch Angel Michael) for being the most fantastic general manager of the restaurants. All my chefs—Ben, Alberto, Cora, Suzanna, Kamil, Ron, Bischal, Jamille, Ausra, Rachel, and Gary, for creating wonderful dishes from my recipes.

Lastly, and above all, I want to thank Peter Gaynor, for being everything...
I love you.